This is the most detailed account of hair pulling and its treatment available anywhere. The authors, a group of internationally known experts, do a valuable public service by educating sufferers and their providers about a disorder that is both more common and more treatable than is widely believed. I only wish I had had this book to recommend to my patients years ago.

> —Lee Baer, Ph.D., Associate Professor of Psychology, Harvard Medical School, author of *Getting Control: Overcoming Your Obsessions and Compulsions*

Help for Hair Pullers *is the definitive book for people who suffer from trichotillomania. Covering the latest knowledge and confronting damaging myths, the authors bring their breadth of clinical and research experience from both the medical and psychological perspectives and create a self-help guide that is a masterpiece. I recommend this book to all who suffer or love someone who suffers from hair pulling. It has the potential to change their lives.*

> —Barbara O. Rothbaum, Ph.D., Associate Professor in Psychiatry and Director, Trauma and Anxiety Recovery Program, Emory University School of Medicine

HELP FOR HAIR PULLERS

ᑊ

Understanding and Coping with Trichotillomania

Nancy J. Keuthen, Ph.D.

Dan J. Stein, M.D.

Gary A. Christenson, M.D.

New Harbinger Publications, Inc.

Publisher's Note

This publication is designed to provide accurate and authoritative information in regard to the subject matter covered. It is sold with the understanding that the publisher is not engaged in rendering psychological, financial, legal, or other professional services. If expert assistance or counseling is needed, the services of a competent professional should be sought.

Distributed in the U.S.A. by Publishers Group West; in Canada by Raincoast Books; in Great Britain by Airlift Book Company, Ltd.; in South Africa by Real Books, Ltd.; in Australia by Boobook; and in New Zealand by Tandem Press.

Copyright © 2001 by Nancy J. Keuthen, Dan J. Stein, and Gary A. Christenson
New Harbinger Publications, Inc.
5674 Shattuck Avenue
Oakland, CA 94609

Cover design by Lightbourne Images
Edited by Angela Watrous
Text design by Michele Waters

Library of Congress Catalog Card Number: 00-134858
ISBN 1-57224-232-9 Paperback

Printed in the United States of America

New Harbinger Publications' Web site address: www.newharbinger.com

03   02   01

10   9   8   7   6   5   4   3   2   1

First printing

Contents

Chapter 3
Stress and Hair Pulling • Hair Pulling and Symbolic
Meanings • Parents and Children • Family History of Hair
Pulling • Serotonin and Other Brain Chemicals • The Basal
Ganglia and Grooming Disorders • Streptococcal Infection
and Hair Pulling

Chapter 4
The Serotonin Reuptake Inhibitors • Side Effects, Doses, and
Durations • Lithium and Naltrexone • Augmentation
Strategies • Managing Side Effects • Should I Be Taking
Medication?

Chapter 5
What Is Behavior Therapy? • How Are Behavioral Principles
Used in Practice? • What Is Cognitive Therapy? • How Does
Cognitive Therapy Work in Practice? • What About
Hypnosis? • What About Psychodynamic Psychotherapy? •
Research to Date • How Do You Choose Among the
Available Treatments?

Chapter 6
Enhancing Motivation • Increasing Awareness • Maintaining
Awareness and Motivation

Chapter 7
Use of Competing Responses • Stimulus Control Techniques
• Setting Goals • Use Of Reinforcement Strategies • Use of
Additional Consequences • Relaxation and Breathing
Techniques • Cognitive Strategies • Relapse Prevention

Chapter 8
Consumer Organizations • Internet Virtual Groups • Dietary
Approaches to Treatment • Finding a Mental Health
Professional • Dealing with Hairdressers • Wigs and
Hairpieces • Friends and Family (To Tell or Not to Tell)

Acknowledgments

We wrote this book to provide understanding and help for those of you who suffer from trichotillomania, a common and, at times, shame-provoking and devastating problem. We attempted to integrate what we have learned from the research literature, our collaborations with colleagues, and our own clinical experiences. We hope that this book will ease your suffering and guide you on your path to recovery.

There are always so many people to thank when completing a task such as this. First and foremost, we wish to recognize and thank all the patients we have worked with over the years. We have appreciated your willingness to share with us the details of your struggles and triumphs with this disorder. You have taught us a lot and it was primarily you who inspired us to take on this challenge.

We would like to recognize the contributions made to this field by Christina Pearson, the Executive Director of the Trichotillomania Learning Center. She has exhibited an unflagging dedication to the advancement of knowledge in this field and the provision of services for all of those who suffer from it. We also wish to acknowledge the invaluable support and intellectual stimulation that we have received from all of our colleagues on the TLC scientific board. In particular, we wish to thank Charles Mansueto, Ph.D., Barbara Rothbaum, Ph.D., and Melinda Stanley, Ph.D., whose independent research and theoretical contributions have advanced the use of cognitive behavioral techniques for this disorder. We would also like to recognize the contributions of the TLC lay board and extend special gratitude to

Jennife Raikes, President of the TLC lay board, who provided invalubale comments on the chapter written for family and friends.

Our editors at New Harbinger Publications, Kristin Beck and Angela Watrous, have made this endeavor a much simpler task than we could ever have anticipated. We are sincerely grateful for their responsiveness, guidance, and support at each stage of the process.

On a more personal note, Dr. Keuthen would like to thank all of her colleagues at the Massachusetts General Hospital, especially those in the Trichotillomania and OCD clinics. She would particularly like to recognize two of her colleagues, Drs. Lee Baer and Michael Jenike, for all of the many ways in which they have provided support and guidance to her over the years. It has been a privilege and an honor to work with them, and she simply can't thank them enough. Lastly, she wishes to express her gratitude to her husband, Bill Fischer, and her parents, Fred and Sophie Keuthen, who have always encouraged her to take on new challenges and sustained an unswerving belief in her abilities.

Dr. Stein would like to thank his colleagues at the MRC Unit on Anxiety Disorders at the University of Stellenbosch, as well as his colleagues at the University of Gainesville, for their generous support and warm collegiality. Heather, Gabriella, and Joshua have always made space for his academic activities, and he owes them an enormous debt of gratitude.

Dr. Christenson would like to thank his mentors, Dr. James Mitchell (Professor and Chairman, Department of Neurosciences, University of North Dakota Medical School) and Dr. Thomas Mackenzie (Professor of Psychiatry, University of Minnesota Medical School), for their guidance and support. He also would like to thank his wife, Janet Christenson, and his parents, Lydon and Ruth Christenson, for all of their support over the years.

Introduction

Over the last few years each of us has seen literally hundreds of patients seeking help for their hair pulling. Who are these people, what are their symptoms, and what are their stories? There is no single answer to these questions. People with hair pulling differ from one another in as many ways as do people without hair pulling. But, to begin, it's useful to share from the lives of two of our patients, Sally, an adult woman, and Jason, a young boy.

The Cases of Sally and Jason

Sally's Story

Sally is a thirty-three-year-old married mother. She works part-time as a consultant in a real estate agency, and spends the rest of her day taking care of her three young children. To those who know her well, she is a "together" person, who has a cheerful and easygoing personality, and is highly devoted to her family. New acquaintances often remark that she could easily be a model given her long, auburn hair, light green eyes, and tall, trim figure.

Sally had never seen a psychiatrist or a psychologist. After all, in many ways her life was a smooth and fulfilling one. There was just one problem. A problem that she had never mentioned to any of her friends. A problem even her husband, Barry, was only dimly aware of. A problem that sometimes kept her awake at night, worrying about whether she was crazy or just plain dumb. A problem that had begun twenty years earlier, when she was a junior at her local high school.

It had all begun shortly after her first menstrual period. While sitting in the bathroom, twirling her long hair and thinking about nothing in particular, she found a hair that was shorter and curlier than the rest. She gripped its base and pulled it out. The hair and root came out with a pleasant "plop." She found herself putting the root to her mouth, licking it, and then biting it off. She even swallowed the root of the hair! A little surprised with herself, she finished her toiletry, and quickly left the bathroom.

From that time forward, Sally rarely had a day of her life during which she did not pull out her hair. Infuriated with herself for this stupid habit, she sometimes managed to keep it down to a few hairs a day. Other times, she gave up fighting it and let her hands attack her scalp, pulling out hundreds of hairs within an hour or two. Now and again, she even pulled hair from her eyebrows or pubic area. She told herself it would be "safe" to pull from the pubic region as it wouldn't be visible to others. Since the age of thirteen, the bald spot on the crown of her head was a constant companion. Sometimes it was only an inch or so, but at other times it grew to five inches in diameter.

When it first started, Sally thought the hair pulling was like nail biting, a habit that she could easily stop if she "really wanted to." Later, though, she admitted that no matter how much she wanted to stop the hair pulling, she simply couldn't. Sally began to think that the hair pulling pointed to a flaw in her character, to a weak will, or to a fundamental inadequacy on her part. It was at this point that she made up her mind never to tell anyone about her self-damaging behavior.

Sure, her spouse knew that she fiddled with her hair a lot. He'd even made comments about how much hair he found on her pillow in the morning. But he'd never known the extent to which she actually pulled out her hair, nor the extent to which she felt ashamed and embarrassed by this behavior. He would have been aghast if he found out that she swallowed the roots of all the hairs she pulled out. He would never have believed that at times she cried herself to sleep after being unable to resist a bad bout of hair pulling.

Sally came for help only after she read a newspaper article about research on hair pulling. She couldn't believe that other people also pulled out their hair. She was further amazed to discover that some of them even bit off the roots of their hair and swallowed them like she did! She doubted that she could be helped, but she was eager to meet a doctor who had spoken to other people with the same problem she had. In addition, she really wouldn't mind talking to one or two individuals who had struggled with trichotillomania like she had for years.

Jason's Story

Jason is a twelve-year-old boy who is an avid fan of baseball and ice hockey. He is the younger brother of Brett, sixteen, and Sarah, fourteen. He enjoys his school, where he hangs out with a close-knit group of friends who share similar interests in sports. They don't pay much attention to the bald spot just over his right ear. They "bought into" Jason's explanation that he had ringworm of the scalp and that the hair would grow back in a little while.

Jason began pulling out his hair when he was eleven years old. He had been playing dares with a kid who lived down the block. "Bet you can't pull out a hair!" said the kid. "Bet I can" he replied. And so he did. And as the hair came out, he experienced a slight thrill of pleasure. His friend had been impressed, so he pulled out another hair. Once again he got that same pleasurable twinge. It was at this point that Jason got hooked. Since then he has pulled out his hair pretty much on a daily basis.

Jason thought to himself that he must be crazy if he pulled out his own hair. He couldn't figure out what made him do it, but it didn't seem like he had any control over it. Particularly if he was involved in a quiet activity, like reading a book or working on his computer, his hand just seemed to automatically start pulling out hair. He never pulled his hair, though, if he was playing a sport or if he was with his friends.

Jason was a pretty self-reliant kid. It never really crossed his mind to talk to anyone about the hair pulling. In fact, he thought it was probably best to keep his secret hidden. His mom would probably get terribly upset if she knew. His dad wouldn't be distressed by it, but he would tell him just to stop. This was advice that he was already giving himself without much success.

Jason was right. When his mom noticed the bald patch, she got fairly upset. She wanted to know how he'd gotten ringworm, and immediately made an appointment with the dermatologist. When the dermatologist asked Jason whether he'd been pulling out his hair, Jason shamefully nodded yes. It was at this point that the dermatologist referred him to a psychiatrist for further evaluation and treatment.

Hair Pulling Is a Hidden but Very Common Problem

Sally, Jason, and many of our other patients have believed that they were the only people in the world who pulled out their hair. They quickly concluded that their behavior was "crazy" and decided to keep it hidden from others. It didn't cross their minds that hair pulling might be common, or that psychiatrists and psychologists may have developed ways to effectively treat this problem.

Perhaps the most important reason we are writing this book is, in fact, to let people with hair pulling know they are not alone. There are many people out there suffering with this very problem. There are also many professionals who are willing and able to help! There is no reason for shame and embarrassment about hair pulling. And there is *every* reason to stop the secrecy and pursue treatment.

How common is hair pulling? A number of large surveys of college students suggest that hair pulling is extremely common. For example, one study found that 1.5 percent of males and 3.4 percent of females had engaged in hair pulling that resulted in visible hair loss (Christenson, Pyle, et al. 1991). Estimates of prevalence are considerably higher, ranging from 13–15 percent, if one includes "nonclinical hair pulling" or hair pulling that does not result in visible hair loss (Stanley et al. 1994). In another study, which reported a hair-pulling rate of 13 percent, only 1 percent of subjects had alopecia (significant hair loss) and 1 percent described associated distress (Rothbaum et al. 1993). Thus, while hair pulling was historically believed to be a rare disorder, recent studies suggest that it is considerably more prevalent than previously thought. These rates exceed those for the more commonly known conditions of schizophrenia, manic depression, and even panic disorder. Indeed, only the most common of conditions, like depression and substance abuse disorders, seem to occur with greater frequency than hair pulling.

This statement would surprise most doctors and lay people. Many family doctors are likely to report that they have never had a patient approach them for help with hair pulling. Dermatologists may remember only one or two cases like Jason's, where a patient with hair loss admitted that their condition was self-inflicted. Even psychiatrists may not often see patients who present with a chief complaint of hair pulling.

There is only one way to make sense of the discrepancy between the high estimated rates of occurrence for this problem and the lack of hair pullers in medical settings. People with hair pulling must be keeping their symptoms to themselves. Most hair pullers are ashamed and embarrassed by their symptoms. They worry that they would be called crazy if anyone knew. So they keep their symptoms hidden, even from medical and mental health professionals. Indeed, a recent survey indicates that only 40 percent of sufferers have received a formal diagnosis (Cohen et al. 1995).

Shame and Embarrassment

The fact that hair pulling is often kept secret from friends, families, and doctors only compounds the shame and embarrassment felt by those who suffer from this condition. People with hair pulling may feel that they are responsible for damaging themselves, and they may worry that professionals will likewise blame them for their behavior.

Not only can hair pulling negatively impact the sense of self, but it may also result in the avoidance of social situations. Thus, in many cases, hair pulling is not simply an annoying habit. Instead, it can cause significant distress and have serious interpersonal consequences.

To complicate matters even further, hair pullers not only suffer from their symptoms, but they also are the perpetrators of their hair pulling. This paradoxical fact may add to the individual's reluctance to pursue treatment. Thus, even though sufferers often feel that they are a victim of their hair pulling, seeking help may be hard given their awareness of their role in the problem. Many also fear that they will be viewed in a similar fashion to other patients who engage in self-mutilative behaviors, such as wrist cutting or skin burning.

The Origins of the Word "Trichotillomania"

The word "trichotillomania" is derived from the Greek words for hair ("trich"), pull ("tillo"), and abnormal love ("mania"). The term was coined by Hallopeau, a French physician who published the first medical report of hair pulling in 1889. Even though this report did not occur until the late nineteenth century, reports of hair pulling existed long before this time.

For example, hair pulling has long been described as a sign of grief, frustration, or emotional turmoil. In the Bible, the prophet Ezra wrote: "And when I heard this thing, I rent my garment and my mantle, and plucked off the hair of my head and of my beard" (Ezra 9:3). In the *Iliad*, Agamemnon was said to groan "from the very deep of his heart" and to tear "many a lock clean forth from his head" (Lang et al. 1945, 165–166). Throughout the centuries numerous writers and artists have depicted people tearing at their hair during difficult times.

Even in the medical literature, references to hair pulling existed long before Hallopeau described his hallmark case. Hippocrates, the famous physician of ancient Greece, advised doctors to routinely assess for hair pulling among other symptoms. He even described a case in which hair pulling was one of many symptoms in a woman suffering from grief.

Why Interest in Trichotillomania Has Grown

During the 1980s, a number of dramatic developments took place in the medical profession's understanding of a condition known as obsessive-compulsive disorder (OCD). In OCD, patients have intrusive, unwanted thoughts (obsessions) that increase anxiety, and repetitive senseless actions (compulsions) designed to relieve this anxiety. For example, thoughts that one is contaminated by dirt or germs can lead to compulsive washing; concerns that one has made a mistake can lead to repetitive checking behaviors; and obsessions about everything having to be in order can lead to compulsive arranging and rearranging.

In OCD, these symptoms are more extreme in severity than for the usual meaning of the word "obsessive" (i.e., overly neat or tidy). People with OCD are tremendously burdened by their symptoms and would give anything for them to disappear. Obsessions and compulsions, which often begin in childhood or adolescence, may be extremely time-consuming, cause significant emotional distress, and may lead to significant problems at home or in the workplace.

Historically, OCD was considered a rare disorder, believed to result from unconscious psychological conflict. The prevailing thought was that it would only respond, if at all, to intensive psychotherapy. A number of recent studies have changed these views completely. First of all, OCD was found to afflict 2–3 percent of the population, suggesting that patients often hide their symptoms and doctors frequently fail to diagnose it. Secondly, OCD was demonstrated to respond to specific medications that affect a brain chemical called serotonin. This led to further research that demonstrated that specific brain chemicals and brain regions play an important role in the disorder.

This work on OCD gradually began to receive more and more attention from the media. Patients with OCD who had responded positively to the newer medications and behavioral treatment came forward to tell their stories on TV and radio. Consumer organizations such as the Obsessive-Compulsive Foundation were established for the purpose of publicizing the disorder and its treatment. Books such as Dr. Judith Rapoport's *The Boy Who Couldn't Stop Washing* (1989) appeared in the popular press and increased awareness of OCD.

As the news about OCD spread to the public, a number of hair pullers wondered whether they had a form of this disorder. At the National Institute of Mental Health, Drs. Judith Rapoport and Susan Swedo, along with their colleagues, embarked on a range of studies to explore hair pulling. In a landmark article in the widely read *New England Journal of Medicine*, these authors published their finding that patients with trichotillomania also responded to one of the medications that was effective for OCD (Swedo et al. 1989). While some similarities in response to medications were reported, some important differences between hair pulling and OCD were also noted. It was at this point that interest in trichotillomania had finally begun to increase.

The Promise of the Future for Hair Pulling

Once trichotillomania had been established as an area of interest for scientific research, the next few years saw the publication of an increasing number of studies on this disorder. In the last few years, the first publications have appeared on the incidence of trichotillomania and its defining features, the rigorous clinical assessment of both adult and child hair pullers, and the underlying neurobiology of this behavior.

In addition, the last several years have seen an increased attention to the treatment of this perplexing problem. There have been the first controlled trials of medication for hair pulling. There has also been increased rigor in the study of psychological treatments for trichotillomania. The research to date provides considerable hope that the future will bring further advances in the treatment of this disorder.

Finally, as occurred for OCD, there has been the rise of a consumer organization exclusively for sufferers of trichotillomania and their families. The Trichotillomania Learning Center, Inc. (TLC) is dedicated to raising public awareness and to providing resources and guidance for sufferers and their families. The TLC also works to raise funding for research and to advance treatment options for clinicians.

How This Book Will Help You

We wrote this book to provide you with answers to your hair-pulling problem. There are literally millions of other people like yourself who suffer from this same disorder. Unfortunately, all too many suffer in silence either because they do not know there is a name for their problem or they are unable to locate a knowledgeable professional in their geographic area. Surprisingly enough, even in some of the major cities in the United States and Europe there are no professionals with the necessary training and experience to treat trichotillomania! This fact, coupled with changes over the past several years in insurance coverage for mental health services, underscored for us the need for a self-help treatment manual.

The good news is that the techniques you are about to learn have proven success in treating trichotillomania. We wrote this book using a step-by-step instructional format to enable you to learn about techniques and then put them into practice using exercises and worksheets. We strongly suggest that you proceed in a systematic fashion, completing one chapter before you proceed to the next, as many of the strategies build on what you have earlier learned. We can't emphasize enough the importance of your active involvement in this treatment program. While knowledge of the disorder alone is helpful, optimal control of hair-pulling urges and behavior will depend on your mastery of the skills presented.

Chapter 1, "Symptoms of Hair Pulling," provides you with an overview of many of the common characteristics of this problem. You will begin to better understand your hair-pulling problem by completing a worksheet assessing different aspects of hair pulling. Subsequently, in chapter 2, "Assessing Your Hair Pulling Pattern," you will determine the severity of your problem and identify your unique hair-pulling triggers. This chapter offers many different exercises to help you map out your hair-pulling picture. Other important areas to assess, including the role of stress, commonly associated problems, family history, and impact on interpersonal functioning are also discussed.

Chapter 3, "What Causes Hair Pulling?," reviews the many different theoretical models used to explain the etiology of this disorder. In chapter 4, "Medications for Hair Pulling," we discuss the most up-to-date recommendations for pharmacological treatment of trichotillomania. Next, in chapter 5, "Psychological Treatments for Hair Pulling," we present the various modalities of psychotherapy that have been used to treat this problem and review empirical evidence for these approaches. The worksheet entitled "Identifying Factors Important for Treatment Selection" will help you consider the pros and cons of medications and different psychological approaches.

Chapter 6, "Starting to Use Behavior Therapy Techniques," will guide you through a series of exercises that will increase and maintain your motivation to address your hair pulling. You will also learn ways to develop and maintain greater awareness of hair-pulling urges and early steps in your hair-pulling behavior. In chapter 7, "Getting Behavioral Techniques to Work for You," you will be introduced to a wide selection of behavioral tools that can effectively control your hair pulling. For each technique, one or more exercises are included that will help you apply and practice these skills.

Chapter 8, "Other Kinds of Help," explores alternative avenues for help ranging from consumer organizations to dietary approaches to Internet groups. Issues in the identification and selection of a therapist are discussed. This chapter also offers tips on how to deal with others (such as hairdressers) and how to decide whether or not to share your problem with friends and family. For those of you with involved family or friends, chapter 9, "Advice for Families and Friends," offers some concrete suggestions on how others can provide help and support. Lastly, chapter 10, "Children with Hair Pulling," provides an overview of our current knowledge including the onset, causes, assessment, and treatment of children, as well as advice for parents.

There is no one treatment formula that will suit every hair puller. Our format will guide you in understanding the unique features of your hair-pulling pattern and assist you in selecting those strategies that will work for you. You will find this book helpful whether you are attempting to control your hair pulling on your own or working with a therapist or a non-professional coach.

Summary Points

➤ Some of the earliest descriptions of hair pulling date back to doctors in ancient Greece.

➤ The term "trichotillomania" is derived from the Greek words for hair ("trich"), pull ("tillo"), and abnormal love ("mania").

➤ Hair pulling is often more than an annoying habit; it may result in significant distress, shame, and embarrassment, and may tremendously impact the lives of sufferers.

➤ The prevalence of this disorder is much higher than previously thought, affecting many millions of Americans at any one time.

➤ Advances in our scientific understanding of obsessive-compulsive disorder (OCD) set the stage for research on trichotillomania.

➤ Considerable help and support now exist for those suffering from trichotillomania. There is no reason for shame and embarrassment and every reason to stop the secrecy and pursue treatment.

➤ Understanding your individual hair-pulling pattern, improved awareness of the behavior, and use of self-control strategies can significantly reduce your hair-pulling problem. This book provides you with the tools you'll need to accomplish these tasks.

Chapter 1

Symptoms of
Hair Pulling

Who Develops Hair Pulling?

Hair pulling can occur in men and women of all ages. However, certain individuals appear to be at greater risk for developing this problem. Historically it has been believed that hair pulling is more likely to occur in females than in males. This idea is supported by several large-scale, recent studies, which consistently find that approximately 70 to 90 percent of hair pullers are female.

Nevertheless, there has been considerable speculation that hair pulling may be more common in men than is appreciated. Men may be less likely to seek treatment for hair pulling, as is the case for most medical and psychological conditions in general. Since most hair-pulling studies have been conducted on patients seeking treatment, rather than the general public, many male hair pullers may be missed.

Furthermore, it has been suggested that men may be able to camouflage their hair pulling more easily than women. A spotty beard or moustache is easily shaved and a missing patch of hair from the top of the head can mimic the male pattern of natural balding. As mentioned earlier, one large survey of college freshman found that 1.5 percent of men and 3.4 percent of women have had significant hair pulling at some point in their lives (Christenson, Pyle, et al.

1991). Thus, although women were still overrepresented, this study suggests that men pull out hair more often than is generally believed.

When Fred came into our office for help, he was extremely distressed by the fact that he pulled out his eyelashes. What made it even worse for him was that he had read about this problem in an article entitled "Women Who Hurt Themselves" in a popular women's magazine. He immediately concluded that this was a "female" problem and worried what it meant about him that he pulled out his hair. He admitted that he had put off seeking help for years because he thought it only happened to women and feared that the doctor would think he was a "freak of nature." His psychiatrist quickly reassured him that while hair pulling occurs more often in females, it occurs in males as well. In fact, as Fred found out, there are millions of men in the world who pull hair from some site on their body.

Hair pulling can develop at any age. This problem has been observed in infants barely one year old, as well as in adults in their sixth or seventh decade of life. However, hair pulling is most likely to begin in late childhood and early adolescence. Studies have been remarkably consistent in noting that the average age of hair pulling onset is around twelve to thirteen years of age.

Previously professionals thought that the onset of hair pulling was typically associated with the experience of some kind of loss. Many different losses have been proposed to be associated with the development of hair pulling. Included among these are:

- death of a close relative or friend

- family break up from a divorce

- loss of companionship due to a geographic move

- decrease in attention received due to the birth of a sibling

- loss of health due to sickness

- loss of mobility due to confinement in a hospital or other setting

Leaving home to attend college is another time when hair pulling can occur in young adults. Perhaps this can reflect the loss of friends, family support, and material comforts.

More recent observations, while occasionally noting an association between hair pulling and loss, suggest that hair pulling can just as often begin without any obvious stress. Occasionally it has been noted to occur after a benign incident draws attention to the hair. Our patients have shared with us a number of rather innocent events that occurred when they began to pull. For example, Sarah began to pull out her hair after she was instructed to bring a hair into her science class to view it under a microscope. Daniella recalls entering a contest with her friend over who had the longest hair, the winner to be determined by a comparison of pulled hairs. Several eyelash pullers have told us that their hair pulling began after they heard that wishing on an eyelash blown from one's finger was as effective in granting desires as wishing on a "falling star." Unfortunately, these sufferers then began to pull out many more lashes to take advantage of this notion!

Occasionally, hair pulling begins soon after some injury to the scalp or hair. Singed hair or scalp, perhaps due to a bad permanent or playing with matches, may bring undue attention to the hair and eventually lead to hair pulling. Similarly, different medical conditions of the scalp that result in scabbing lesions can also lead to hair pulling. An initial bout of scalp lice also resulted in the beginning of this behavior for several of our patients.

Modeling, or the mimicking of behavior observed in another, may also account for why some children begin to pull out their hair. A number of our patients recall beginning to pull out hair shortly after they saw a friend, sibling, or parent doing this. Several mothers have told us that they finally sought out help, not because of great concern about their own behavior, but because they were beginning to see their children play with their hair after seeing "mommy do the same." Modeling may be one reason why hair pulling has been observed within multiple family members, although genetic influences may also play a role (this will be discussed further in chapter 3).

An early account of hair pulling supports the power of modeling. An epidemic of hair loss was observed in an orphanage for girls (Davis 1914). Never having heard of trichotillomania, the reporting physician suspected that the hair loss was infectious in nature and treated it accordingly. However, there were several characteristics of the spread of the "illness," as well as response to treatment, that were inconsistent with his initial diagnosis. A second epidemic within the same orphanage, coupled with the physician's newfound awareness of the syndrome of trichotillomania, led him to conclude that the hair loss represented trichotillomania spread by modeling. The behavior was then believed to be reinforced by the extra attention that the "sick" girls received.

Onset of menses has been suggested as another precipitant of hair pulling in women by a number of investigators. Certainly, the average age of onset for hair pulling is very close to the usual time of menses. Nevertheless, our anecdotal impression is that when individual histories are taken, it is rare for hair pulling and menses to have both started within a brief time span. Alternatively, it is possible that those hormonal factors that contribute to the onset of menses may also play a role in precipitating hair pulling.

In summary, a broad array of events appear to impact those individuals who develop hair pulling. However, we have been impressed by the fact that most hair pullers cannot identify any one event that appears to have precipitated their trichotillomania. As for many disorders, perhaps there are developmental and physiological reasons that predispose people to begin hair pulling at commonly observed ages (see chapter 3 for further discussion of this topic).

Where Do People Pull Hair From?

Virtually any body hair can become a target for pulling in trichotillomania. Scalp hair is the most common hair site and may lead to several patterns of hair loss. Most frequently observed are patches of hair loss from the very top of the head, a pattern that has been referred to as the "tonsure" pattern or, more descriptively, the "Friar Tuck sign." Hair loss from areas over the ears is also quite common. Hair pulling from the very back of the head is somewhat less typical. Hair loss may be confined to a specific area across time, or may vary with time, sometimes in an attempt by the patient to avoid complete baldness in one area. It may vary from mild thinning to complete baldness. There may also be a patchy distribution or a more defined linear, circular, or oval area.

The most common hair-pulling regions in descending order of frequency are:

- scalp

- eyelashes

- eyebrows

- pubic hair

- facial hair

Arm, leg, and chest hair are less common but can also occur. Even nasal, ear, and hair around the anus is extracted by some pullers.

Sarah initially came in for help admitting that she had a problem with pulling hair from her scalp. Unfortunately, at that time her therapist failed to complete a detailed history of her hair pulling. Sarah's therapy became quickly focused on how the hair pulling impacted her relationships, especially the effect that it had on her on-again, off-again relationship with her boyfriend. It was only several months later that Sarah found the courage to tell her therapist that she also plucked out all the hairs from her pubic region. This really disturbed her, as she wondered whether this indicated something about her sexuality. At this point her therapy quickly refocussed on her feelings about her sexuality.

It was many months later that Sarah read in an article on trichotillomania that pulling hair from the pubic area is not uncommon. Furthermore, she read that not all professionals believed that pulling from this area had any relationship to one's sexuality. In fact, some endorsed explanations as simple as the fact that a bald patch in this area would be less obvious and result in less shame and embarrassment, thus making it a preferred pulling site for some individuals.

A few of our patients have reported pulling hair from a partner or child. Hair pulling from pets and inanimate objects (e.g., dolls or stuffed animals) has also been reported. One of our younger patients, Jane, an eleven-year-old girl, sheepishly admitted to us that she had tried on several occasions to pull out the whiskers from her cat. Not surprisingly, this was something that her cat had not taken to at all kindly! She went on to explain that the whiskers stuck out so far that it felt to her as if they were too long, and that bothered her. She continued to try to do this from time to time until the day the cat let out a loud yelp and her secret was discovered by her mother. It was at this point that her parents brought her into us for professional evaluation. In cases where a child has not been seen pulling his or her own hair and has denied hair pulling, an "epidemic" of hair loss from dolls and toys may give a clue to the real source of the child's hair loss.

Loose blanket fibers, blades of grass, or other similar fibrous materials have also been reported as targets for extraction by some pullers. Some of our patients have obtained wigs to disguise hair loss from pulling, only to subsequently pull hair from the hairpiece.

Most people with hair pulling pull from between two and three sites, possibly a combination of scalp and lashes, or of lashes and brows. Each hair pulling region often has its own history in regards to the person's age at the time of onset and course. It's not atypical for one area to have been a problem in the past, only to resolve while another hair-pulling site develops or continues to persist.

Trichophagy: The Eating of Hair

Although hair that has been pulled out may simply be discarded, hair pullers often continue to examine or play with the loose strands. The person may inspect the hair closely, trying to determine whether the hair root is intact. For many people with hair pulling this is a critical part of the hair pulling sequence. Many will report that a hair pull isn't right unless the extracted hair has an intact root. The hair may be rolled between the fingers or the root may be bitten off. On very rare occasions, people may save their pulled hair. In fact, one patient told us that she used the hairs she pulled out for dental floss!

Another very typical behavior following hair pulling is the manipulation of the hair with the mouth. In one large series of female hair pullers, one-third of the individuals were reported to bite or chew off bits of hair, often at the bulb end, immediately after hair extraction (Christenson, MacKenzie, et al. 1991). In many cases, the hair was then discarded. In several cases, however, continued chewing resulted in the complete destruction of the hair. Fifty percent of all hair pullers had some oral component to their hair pulling, such as running the hair along one's lips, licking the hair, or some other manner of mouthing the hair.

About one in ten patients describe complete ingestion of at least some of their hair. The technical term for eating hair is *trichophagy*. Although such behavior may result in nothing more severe than embarrassment, in some cases it can lead to serious medical consequences (as described later in this chapter).

How Long Does Hair Pulling Persist?

The question of how long hair pulling continues has not been well studied. This reflects the fact that research on trichotillomania, for the most part, is only a recent phenomenon. Most studies so far have only looked at hair pulling from a cross-sectional point of view. In other words, researchers have studied what is characteristic about a group of people with hair pulling within a very short time frame, rather than following the same group over time in a longitudinal fashion.

Although some investigators have asked people about the natural course of their hair pulling, information collected in this way is always vulnerable to errors in recall. Those studies that have followed hair pullers over time have not collected information about the natural course of the behavior since they have all focused on attempts to treat the problem. Furthermore, such studies have generally been conducted over time periods of less than a year.

Perhaps the most significant limitation in our current knowledge of the natural course of trichotillomania is that studies have only looked at those who are currently pulling hair. Those people who were able to stop their pulling without medical or psychological intervention remain a silent, but potentially valuable, source of information about other outcomes of hair pulling different from those typically seen in treatment facilities.

The previous points notwithstanding, hair pulling is generally thought to be a chronic condition, particularly if it continues into adulthood. Some clinicians and researchers suggest that this may not be so with very young hair pullers. They even argue for a distinct type of the disorder known as "early onset" trichotillomania. This form of the disorder has been described as having a more equal gender ratio as well as a greater tendency to be self-limited.

Although the suggestion exists that some childhood hair pulling may be completely outgrown, we have been impressed by the number of adults who report a temporary resolution of hair pulling in childhood, only to be followed by a relapse later on in life. In such cases there is often a reluctance to return to their former health care providers, or a decision to hide the consequences of their behavior with wigs, makeup, and other methods of disguise. In such cases it is easy to imagine that the treating physician or psychologist would conclude that the patient's problem had permanently resolved. Clearly, researchers need to devote far more attention toward studying the many factors involved in the onset of trichotillomania, as well as its resolution or continuation.

One recent paper provides some hope regarding treatment outcome with this disorder (Keuthen et al. 1998). Sixty-three hair pullers who received state-of-the-art treatment in a specialty clinic at Massachusetts General Hospital were studied. On average, three and a half years elapsed between initial evaluation in clinic and the time of follow-up evaluation. Significant improvements were reported to occur over time in hair pulling, depression, anxiety, self-esteem, and psychosocial functioning. These results offer hope that many hair pullers can obtain relief with appropriate treatment. However, future research needs to study these individuals for longer follow-up periods to see if these treatment benefits continued over time.

Other Associated Behaviors

Many hair pullers also exhibit other "nervous habits." Some of these include nail and cuticle biting, knuckle biting or cracking, finger sucking, face or scalp picking, acne or scab picking, tongue chewing or biting, nose picking, skin scratching, clothes picking, lip biting or twisting, body rocking, bruxism or jaw clenching, cheek chewing, and head banging.

The relationship between hair pulling and these other behaviors is unclear, and may vary from case to case. For example, it has been reported that treatment of thumb sucking in children can lead to termination of the hair pulling. Alternatively, other researchers have reported that successful treatment for trichotillomania or nail biting can be associated with the onset of the other habit. Many of the same techniques that you will learn later on in this book to help with your hair pulling can also be effective for treatment of these other habits if no medical etiology exists for them.

Skin picking is a habit that deserves particular mention here, as it often has many features in common with hair pulling. It is also a repetitive, unwanted behavior that can cause physical damage. It often begins in childhood or adolescence and may also be more common in women. People with skin picking can report gratification when they remove a scab. This is similar to the same feeling that hair pullers may have when they remove an unwanted hair. Skin pickers similarly report significant shame and embarrassment, at times coupled with interference in their lives. It is also not unusual for hair pullers to pick at those specific sites from which they pull hair. Skin picking can also be common in obsessive-compulsive disorder (OCD) and related disorders. Not surprisingly, skin picking may respond to many of the behavioral techniques we present in this book, as well as to some of the same medications used to treat hair pulling.

Mary told us that her skin picking initially began as part of her hair pulling. She particularly liked to pull out the roots of her hair. She had a habit of holding a root up to the light and then sometimes chewing it off. In order to make sure that the root came out, she would sometimes dig a little into her scalp with her nails. She found that pulling off the scab that formed was also associated with a pleasurable feeling, and she began to do this on a regular basis as well. When she later learned the techniques of habit reversal to help her stop her hair pulling, she realized that the same tools could help her to stop her scab picking at the same time.

It has historically been questioned whether trichotillomania is a self-injurious behavior and, thus, whether other self-destructive behaviors occur along with hair pulling. Unpublished data from a large sample of hair pullers collected by one of the authors (DJS) indicates that only 6.9 percent of patients have ever purposefully cut themselves and only 3.2 percent have attempted to burn themselves. Suicide attempts were reported for 15.1 percent of the sample, though this should be interpreted keeping in mind the high rate of co-occurring depression in hair pullers. Thus, this behavior may not be associated with the hair pulling per se, but rather with the depression that can often co-occur in those individuals who suffer from hair pulling.

Now that you are familiar with the different clinical features that can be present in hair pulling, as well as other associated behaviors, take a minute to complete the following exercise. It will help you to further specify the unique features of your hair pulling habit as well as other similar behaviors.

Exercise:
Identifying Your Hair-Pulling Picture

Use the following worksheet to help you identify the various characteristics of your own hair-pulling problem. Be as honest with yourself
as you can. Try not to be embarrassed—no one else needs to see
this sheet other than yourself!

Age of onset: _____

For the category below, please circle those items that apply to you
and describe.

Factors associated with onset of hair pulling:

Traumatic loss: _____

_____

_____

Modeling by others: _____

_____

_____

Specific event (e.g., a dare, science class): _____

_____

_____

Onset of menses: _____

_____

_____

Medical condition: _____

_____

_____

Other psychological problem: _____

_____

_____

_____

For each of the following categories, circle all of the items that apply and write "C" for current and "P" for past.

Site(s) of pulling:

> Scalp ___
>
> Eyelashes ___
>
> Eyebrows ___
>
> Pubis ___
>
> Face ___
>
> Arm/Leg ___
>
> Chest ___
>
> Other (describe): _____

Hair pulling from other sources:

> Partner ___
>
> Child ___
>
> Sibling ___
>
> Friend ___
>
> Pet ___
>
> Doll or stuffed animal ___
>
> Other (describe): _____

Method of Hair Extraction:

> Pulling with fingers ___
>
> Rubbing hair ___
>
> Tweezers ___
>
> Other (please describe): _____

Oral behaviors associated with hair pulling:

> Lick hair ___
>
> Rub along lips ___
>
> Bite off root ___
>
> Chew hair into small pieces ___
>
> Swallow hair ___

Other (please describe): _____

Disposition of extracted hair:

      Visual inspection of hair ____

      Oral behaviors ____

      Play with loose hair in fingers ____

      Save hair ____

      Discard hair ____

      Other (please describe): _____

Other associated behaviors:

      Nail or cuticle biting ____

      Knuckle biting or cracking ____

      Finger sucking ____

      Face picking ____

      Scalp picking ____

      Acne or scab picking ____

      Tongue chewing or biting ____

      Nose picking ____

      Skin scratching ____

      Clothes picking ____

      Lip biting or twisting ____

      Body rocking ____

      Bruxism or jaw clenching ____

      Cheek chewing ____

      Head banging ____

Course of hair pulling (circle the one answer which most applies to you):

      No periods without hair pulling since onset

      Some periods early on without hair pulling but now continuous pulling

      Current episodes of pulling as well as periods without hair pulling

Psychological Effects of Hair Pulling

One of the most important effects of hair pulling is the lowering of self-esteem. Although self-esteem problems may be present in depression and other associated conditions, people with hair pulling describe lowered self-esteem directly related to their inability to control their behavior, or as a result of their actual hair loss.

The effect of hair pulling on self-esteem has only recently been studied. People who pull out their hair were reported to have medium levels of self-esteem according to the score ranges on a self-esteem scale (Soriano et al. 1996). Surprisingly, neither duration of hair pulling, severity of hair loss, or age of onset greatly influenced the degree of self-esteem. However, lower self-esteem was found to be associated with depressed mood and anxiety, the frequency of hair pulling, and overall dissatisfaction with body appearance separate from their hair. Clearly, further understanding of this important psychological complication of hair pulling is sorely needed.

Contributing to the self-esteem issue is the frequent scolding and shaming that can come from parents, partners, or friends. Hair pullers are often given the simplistic advice of "just stop doing it" without any understanding from the individual of just how difficult a task this can be. In fact, people with hair pulling have often already resorted unsuccessfully to their own home remedies including wearing gloves or Band-Aids on their hands, cutting their nails, covering their heads, sitting on their hands (or even tying a hand down). People with hair pulling may blame themselves for their "weakness" in not being able to cure themselves. Embarrassment about their behavior can, in some cases, also lead to denial that they pull. When this occurs, it can lead to unnecessary doctor visits and tests in an effort to determine the reason for hair loss or, conversely, to an avoidance of seeking help from health professionals.

Fear of embarrassment or concern about the perceptions of others may lead people with hair pulling to avoid circumstances in which their problem could be discovered. Common situations that may be avoided include windy conditions, swimming, overnight visits, hair cuts/styling, and sex. People may avoid checkups with their physician, and, in the case of pubic hair pulling, annual pelvic exams. Pullers may also avoid opthalmalogists if they pull eyelashes or eyebrows, and dentists if they chew the extracted hair. Sufferers may also avoid enjoyable activities such as reading or watching television when they know that such activities trigger their hair pulling. Avoidance may lead to even further loss of self-esteem and isolation. Therefore, therapy for trichotillomania should not only focus on the hair-pulling behavior, but also on the psychological impact of suffering from the disorder.

Medical Complications of Hair Pulling

Trichotillomania can result in several medical problems. The most obvious is damage to the hair or skin at the site of hair pulling. Hair pulling can lead to short- or long-term damage to the hair follicle. This leads to a characteristic profile on microscopic examination of a sample of skin (skin biopsy), which differentiates trichotillomania from other causes of hair loss. Fortunately, such scalp biopsies are rarely required when someone with trichotillomania comes for treatment. However, in cases in which the patient is too young or too embarrassed to reveal the true source of hair loss, this diagnostic procedure may be beneficial.

Damage to the hair follicle can cause changes in the feel or appearance of hair regrowth. It is not uncommon for hair to turn gray or whiten more quickly in areas of hair pulling. Unfortunately, the hair may not revert to its natural color even after a hair puller gains control over the problem. Hair coloring offers a simple and usually acceptable solution in such cases. Textural changes may also occur. Hair regrowth can be coarse, thick, or kinky, which may then contribute to even more pulling. With protracted pulling, entire patches of curly hair may appear in a scalp of normally straight hair.

Hair follicle damage and/or skin damage from digging or scratching with fingers or tweezers during the course of hair pulling can lead to infections. Scabbing over of these wounds often leads to yet another thing to pick and pull at, setting up a vicious cycle of further scratching and pulling. As reported earlier, picking at lesions on the scalp or other body sites occurs in a high proportion of hair pullers.

Hair biting, gnawing, and ingestion can lead to yet another group of dental and medical problems. Although apparently rare, some of our patients have described gum disease resulting from the frequent pulling of hair between their teeth. Actual enamel erosion has also been reported to occur from the constant grinding of pulled hair. If hair is ingested, particularly long strands, a person can develop a hairball, or *trichobezoar*, similar to those that develop in cats and cows. These can grow so large as to fill the entire hollow of the stomach before they are diagnosed. There have even been several accounts of patients developing trichobezoars that not only filled the entire stomach but ran the length of the entire small intestine as well (given the rather morbid name of the "Rapunzel syndrome").

Symptoms of trichobezoars include loss of appetite, stomach upset, weakness, weight loss, vomiting, and diarrhea or constipation. Complications of these hair balls include poor absorption resulting in iron and vitamin B_{12} deficiencies, anemia from bleeding, stomach and bowel obstruction, perforation of the stomach or intestines, abdominal infection, and even death. Fortunately, our clinical experience suggests that these are quite rare. In the over three hundred patients we have seen together we have encountered only one case of trichobezoar. However, a recent study of a group of children and adolescent hair pullers in India found over 38 percent had a trichobezoar or *trichophytobezoar* (made up of both hair and vegetable matter) when they were examined extensively for such problems (Bhatia et al. 1991). Most had no or only mild symptoms suggestive of a stomach or intestinal problem. We therefore encourage clinicians to always inquire about hair eating and for people to volunteer this information when seeking help.

The physical act of hair pulling may also have other medical consequences. Patients have shown us finger calluses that resulted from years of pulling. Other pullers have reported cuts developing from a firm, quick pull of a hair that didn't readily come out. Repetitive hair pulling can lead to temporary muscle fatigue which may inadvertently be beneficial in leading a hair puller to stop a hair pulling episode earlier than he or she might have otherwise. Repeated hair pulling has even resulted in carpal tunnel syndrome, a wrist disorder that has gained notoriety as a frequent consequence of the repetitive use of computer keyboards (O'Sullivan et al. 1996).

Summary Points

➤ Hair pulling can occur in individuals of either gender at any age.

➤ Although believed to occur more often in women, this may reflect the reluctance of men to seek help.

► Hair pulling usually begins in late childhood or early adolescence.

► Hair can be pulled from any body site. Scalp hair is most commonly pulled, with eyelashes, eyebrows, and pubic hair not uncommonly pulled. Less often, hair is pulled from other people or from inanimate objects.

► In 50 percent of hair pullers, an oral habit is associated with the hair extraction. These may include eating the hair (trichophagy) or rubbing it along the lips. A rare medical complication of hair pulling is an intestinal hairball (trichobezoar).

► Hair pulling is often a chronic problem and may lead to lowered self-esteem, embarrassment, or avoidance of various social situations. Hair pulling can have a significant impact on the lives of sufferers.

Chapter 2

Assessing Your Hair-Pulling Pattern

Understanding your unique hair-pulling pattern is your first step toward achieving control over your problem. Hair pullers can extract hair from any body part and different individuals often pull from different places. Sometimes the same hair puller may even change the site(s) and pattern of his or her hair pulling over time. In light of this, it's important that you discover your "signature pattern" of hair pulling so that you can best manage it.

Many hair pullers think that they already know their signature pattern of hair pulling. Only when they do some of the following exercises do they realize that there are aspects to their hair pulling of which they are unaware. Just like your handwritten signature, hair pulling can become an automatic behavior. Often when behaviors become automatic, we lose our conscious awareness of the many separate steps in the process. Pretend that you would like to verbally describe your handwritten signature in as much detail as necessary for a visually impaired person to copy it. You need to be able to describe your hair pulling in similar detail so that you can gain the control over it that you desire.

While some hair pullers can pull nearly every day, others can go for days without urges or pulls, only to later extract large amounts of hair in a "binge-like" pattern. Some hair pullers seek hair that has a certain texture or color. Others pull for the physical sensations accompanying the behavior or the emotional consequences of pleasure, gratification, or relief. Still other hair pullers will purposefully extract hair to create symmetry in their eyebrows or eyelashes. Our clinical experience in treating hundreds of hair pullers has shown that those individuals who are dedicated to ongoing assessment are more likely to be successful in achieving mastery over their hair-pulling behavior.

Accurate assessment of your hair pulling before, during, and after treatment is important for the following reasons:

- Assessing the severity of your hair pulling gives you a baseline picture of the nature and extent of your problem.

- Monitoring your hair pulling, in conjunction with its associated triggers, provides you with the information you need to design an individualized self-help plan.

- Ongoing assessment during treatment measures your success in controlling your symptoms.

- Repeated assessment over time helps you stay motivated and focused on your individual goals.

In this chapter we will present several different ways to help you in the assessment of your hair pulling. All of these methods will provide you with significant amounts of information about your hair-pulling pattern. You can use these techniques on your own without the assistance of a trained professional. These methods are, for the most part, complementary, and we recommend using as many of them as you can. We encourage use of these methods on an ongoing basis throughout your self-help treatment program.

One important reminder: Hair pulling is a "waxing and waning" problem. By this we mean that it is not unusual for hair pulling symptoms to change from day to day. Therefore, when you assess your problem, you should expect fluctuations in the numbers of hairs pulled on a daily basis. This will be important when you attempt to get an accurate baseline, as well as when you try to measure improvement with treatment.

Let's discuss two examples that will help to demonstrate this last point. Women who experience fluctuations in their hair pulling as a function of their menstrual cycle will report different daily hair pulling counts at different times in their cycle. If a woman had the most common pattern of premenstrual worsening in her hair pulling, she would likely overestimate her baseline rate if she measured it only during her premenstrual week. Similarly, hair pullers would be less likely to be successful in their attempts to control their hair pulling if they encountered unusual stress. Thus, if an adverse event happens during treatment efforts, you should expect possible worsening in hair-pulling counts despite efforts at control. Because of this, it would be most helpful for you to do your initial assessment during a time that is most representative of your hair-pulling pattern. Additionally, you should expect some fluctuations in your hair-pulling counts once you embark on treatment, despite your efforts at symptom control.

Now let's start to unravel the pattern of your own hair pulling by doing some exercises. You should feel good about yourself since you have made the commitment to work on your hair pulling. We all know that it's hard to face challenges, especially when we're not sure how well we will do. Try to remember the following two things:

- You won't know if you can control your hair pulling unless you try.

- Your hair pulling is unlikely to change unless you try.

Assessing Hair-Pulling Severity

One of the first steps in starting your self-help journey is to document how severe your hair-pulling problem is prior to your self-help efforts. There are many different ways to do this. We recommend that you use several, if not all, of these methods. You're likely to find that the more effort you put into the assessment process, the better your treatment outcome will be.

Self-Monitoring Frequency of Hair Pulling

An important method of assessment is *self-monitoring*, which involves keeping records of your hair pulling. Often this is done in combination with entries for associated triggers for hair pulling (e.g., specific situations, emotions, sensations, motor behaviors, and associated thoughts), though initially we will focus on simply recording the occurrence of the actual hair pulling.

This technique can be time-consuming and inconvenient, but the results are well worth it! Initially you may find it difficult to keep self-monitoring records. Once you have done it for a while, you will find that it becomes familiar and much easier to do. Many patients view self-monitoring as the foundation of their behavioral treatment plan.

Additional self-monitoring tasks later in the chapter provide you with the necessary information you will need to design an effective, individualized plan of intervention. In the absence of this information, most treatment plans are considerably less effective, as they do not sufficiently address the relevant targets for your hair pulling. By monitoring the actual hair pulling and related cues, you are taking your first steps toward controlling the problem that has had control over you!

Self-monitoring of hair pulling often has the unexpected benefit of reducing the actual number of hairs pulled. This represents the clinical phenomenon called *behavioral reactivity*. This refers to a decrease in the occurrence of a negative behavior when one records its occurrence. Thus, by being careful in your self-monitoring, you will have likely already started on the path to decreasing your hair pulling.

Exercise: Weekly Hair-Pulling Record

One of the simplest ways to assess severity is to record the number of hairs extracted. You can accomplish this goal simply with the use of paper and pencil, or you can use instrumentation such as a golf counter. In the *tic-toc method* you make a mark on a recording sheet throughout the day every time that you pull. Recorded lines are generally grouped in clusters of five with the fifth entry diagonally intersecting the prior four vertical marks. It is crucial that you make the entry as soon after you pulled the hair as possible, as you will tend to underreport symptoms if you try to remember them at a later time. Some hair pullers, especially students, find it helpful to keep a Post-it note on the inside of a book or notebook for their daily count. Later in the day they transcribe their hair-pulling counts to their weekly recording sheets.

Other hair pullers like to use a golf counter for recording purposes. These devices are small enough to easily fit into a pocket or purse. They can be purchased at many sporting goods stores and are quite inexpensive and simple to use. You just click the counter after every hair that you extract. At the end of the day you then copy the hair-pulling tally into your record.

For the next seven days, use the tic-toc method or a golf counter to accurately record every hair pull. At the end of each day, record your daily total on the self-monitoring hair-pulling record below. At the end of the week, sum the daily totals to get your weekly tally. Remember: You don't have to make an entry on your

record if you do not extract the hair, which may function as an
incentive for you to resist pulling your hair out.

Self-Monitoring Hair-Pulling Record

(Week of _____ to _____)

Sunday   ____

Monday   ____

Tuesday   ____

Wednesday   ____

Thursday   ____

Friday   ____

Saturday   ____

Weekly Total   ____

Now that you have collected data on the numbers of hair that you
pull, let's proceed to the next exercise that will help you display the
results of your monitoring.

Exercise: Graphing Your Daily Hair Pulls

Next we suggest you complete the graph below to illustrate your
hair-pulling behavior over time. This task is a useful way to visually
document fluctuations in your baseline hair-pulling counts, as well
as track your improvement once you start treatment. Many hair pullers find it rewarding to continue graphing throughout this process so
that they are able to see their actual progress on paper. If you wish
to do so, you may want to make several photocopies of this graph
before you begin.

The horizontal axis indicates successive days during your monitoring period (e.g., Day 1, Day 2, Day 3). For the vertical axis, you will need to decide how many hairs each block represents (e.g., 1, 5, 10, 15, 20, 25, etc.). To figure this out you should first estimate the range of your daily hair loss. Then divide your highest daily hair-pull count by the number of blocks on this axis (10). For example, if you frequently pull up to 150 hairs each day, 150 hairs ÷ 10 = 15 hairs per block. Now calculate it for yourself and fill in the numbers on the vertical axis. For the example we gave, it would be 15, 30, 45, 60, etc.). Once you complete this calculation and write the numbers on the vertical axis, graph the daily hair-pull counts and connect the points.

Collecting Extracted Hairs

Another way to assess the severity of hair pulling is to collect and count all the hairs that you extract from your body. While we prefer that you assess severity using the more labor-intensive self-monitoring techniques described above, collecting pulled hairs can be useful for those individuals who will not record actual counts upon hair extraction, or who have already completed several weeks of this exercise. This technique may also provide a more accurate count of hair pulls, particularly when binges occur and the hair puller is reluctant to stop to record the behavior. For those hair pullers who normally chew or ingest the hair, this technique may have the additional benefit of decreasing this potentially dangerous behavior.

Many hair pullers find it aversive to look at the collection of hairs extracted from their body. Some hair pullers decrease their hair pulling to avoid seeing the physical evidence of their hair-pulling habit. This task is not designed to be punitive or distasteful. Rather, it is developed to help you acquire control over your hair-pulling habit. Prominent display of the extracted hairs can also be a useful technique to maintain awareness and motivation. The next exercise will instruct you in how to go about collecting your extracted hairs.

Exercise: Collecting Extracted Hairs

Buy either a box of envelopes or get a clear glass container. Try to collect all the hairs that you pull and keep them in the envelope or the jar for the day. At the end of the day count up all the hairs. You may find it helpful to use tweezers to count the individual hairs. You can use the same hair-pulling record and graph used earlier to record your daily tally and plot your hair-pulling frequency.

Rating Hair-Pulling Severity with a Self-Report Scale

Another self-help assessment method is the use of a self-rated scale. This is a paper-and-pencil form that you can complete by yourself. Several scales are available for the assessment of hair pulling, although only one self-report scale has been developed exclusively for use by the hair puller alone to measure symptom severity (Keuthen et al. 1995).

This scale requires only a few minutes each time that you complete it. Comparison of your ratings over time will give you feedback as to how your hair pulling has changed. Since it will take a while before the physical damage of your hair pulling is gone, these scales can help identify week-by-week, stepwise improvement. We recommend that you complete this scale once a week during your active self-help treatment, and for several months after you have achieved good control over your hair pulling. This will help you be aware of any changes that occur in your behavior. We will now briefly discuss the hair-pulling severity scale.

The Massachusetts General Hospital (MGH) Hairpulling Scale is a seven-question scale that measures the severity of hair pulling. Individual questions inquire about the frequency and intensity of urges, ability to control urges, frequency of hair pulling, resistance to hair pulling, ability to control hair pulling, and associated distress.

Each item is rated 0 to 4, depending on severity. Comparison of scores on individual scale items reflects changes in these symptoms over time.

Exercise: Rating Hair-Pulling Severity with a Self-Report Scale

Now that you know about the paper-and-pencil self-rating scale, take a minute to complete it and give yourself a baseline rating of your hair-pulling symptoms.

The Massachusetts General Hospital (MGH) Hair Pulling Scale

Name _____ Date _____

Instructions: For each question, pick the one statement in that group which best describes your behaviors and/or feelings over the past week. If you have been having ups and downs, try to estimate an average for the past week. Be sure to read all the statements in each group before making your choice.

For the next three questions, rate only the urges to pull your hair.

1. Frequency of urges. On an average day, how often did you feel the urge to pull your hair?

   0   This week I felt no urges to pull my hair.

   1   This week I felt an occasional urge to pull my hair.

   2   This week I felt an urge to pull my hair often.

   3   This week I felt an urge to pull my hair very often.

   4   This week I felt near constant urges to pull my hair.

2. Intensity of urges. On an average day, how intense or "strong" were the urges to pull your hair?

   0   This week I did not feel any urges to pull my hair.

   1   This week I felt mild urges to pull my hair.

   2   This week I felt moderate urges to pull my hair.

   3   This week I felt severe urges to pull my hair.

   4   This week I felt extreme urges to pull my hair.

3. Ability to control the urges. On an average day, how much control do you have over the urges to pull your hair?

   0   This week I could always control the urges, or I did not feel any urges to pull my hair.

1   This week I was able to distract myself from the urges to pull my hair most of the time.

2   This week I was able to distract myself from the urges to pull my hair some of the time.

3   This week I was able to distract myself from the urges to pull my hair rarely.

4   This week I was never able to distract myself from the urges to pull my hair.

For the next three questions, rate only the actual hair pulling.

4. Frequency of hair pulling. On an average day, how often did you actually pull your hair?

0   This week I did not pull my hair.

1   This week I pulled my hair occasionally.

2   This week I pulled my hair often.

3   This week I pulled my hair very often.

4   This week I pulled my hair so often it felt like I was always doing it.

5. Attempts to resist hair pulling. On an average day, how often did you make an attempt to stop yourself from actually pulling your hair?

0   This week I felt no urges to pull my hair.

1   This week I tried to resist the urge to pull my hair almost all of the time.

2   This week I tried to resist the urge to pull my hair some of the time.

3   This week I tried to resist the urge to pull my hair rarely.

4   This week I never tried to resist the urge to pull my hair.

6. Control over hair pulling. On an average day, how often were you successful at actually stopping yourself from pulling your hair?

0   This week I did not pull my hair.

1   This week I was able to resist pulling my hair almost all of the time.

2   This week I was able to resist pulling my hair most of the time.

3   This week I was able to resist pulling my hair some of the time.

4   This week I was rarely able to resist pulling my hair.

For the last question, rate the consequences of your hair pulling.

7. Associated distress. Hair pulling can make some people feel
   moody, "on edge," or sad. During the past week how uncomfortable did your hair pulling make you feel?

   0   This week I did not feel uncomfortable about my hair pulling.

   1   This week I felt vaguely uncomfortable about my
        hair pulling.

   2   This week I felt noticeably uncomfortable about my
        hair pulling.

   3   This week I felt significantly uncomfortable about my
        hair pulling.

   4   This week I felt intensely uncomfortable about my
        hair pulling.

Source: Keuthen, N. J., R. L. O'Sullivan, J. N. Ricciardi, et al. 1995. "The Massachusetts General Hospital (MGH) Hairpulling Scale, I. Development and factor analysis." *Psychotherapy and Psychosomatics* 64:141–145. Used with permission of
publisher, S. Karger, located in Basel, Switzerland.

You have now completed several exercises that measure the
severity of your hair pulling. In the following section we will focus
on the assessment of factors that occur in association with your hair
pulling and can function as "triggers" for the behavior.

Assessing Hair-Pulling Triggers

Research has shown that hair pulling can be described by two different patterns: automatic or "habitual" pulling versus compulsive or
"binge-like" pulling (Christenson et al. 1993). More hair pullers than
not describe the habitual type as the predominant pattern to their
hair pulling. This fact is not surprising given that the behavior generally develops over time and becomes routinely associated with many
different situations, emotional states, or physical sensations.

In both cases, the hair pulling is associated with specific cues or
triggers. Very often intense emotional states accompany the more
binge-like pattern of pulling. In contrast, sedentary situations (e.g.,
TV, reading, computer), especially those in which the individual is
mentally focused on another activity, often accompany the habitual
pattern of hair pulling.

Before we introduce new tools for coping with hair-pulling triggers, it is essential that you identify the internal and external contexts
in which your hair pulling occurs. The following exercises will assist
you in learning more about when, where, how, and why you pull
your hair.

Exercise: Identifying Your Hair-Pulling Triggers

As discussed above, every hair puller has common cues that routinely precede their hair pulling. These stimuli can be either internal (e.g., thoughts, sensations, motor behaviors, or feelings) or external (e.g., situations or activities). Identification and awareness of these triggers is necessary before you can decide how to intervene to minimize your pulling. One way to accomplish this task is for you to review the following checklist and identify those items that characterize your pulling. We do not anticipate that all of your triggers will be listed. It is likely that you will be able to generate some other cues that you frequently encounter. You may need to close your eyes and visualize past hair-pulling episodes to assist you in identification of your triggers.

Checklist of Common Hair-Pulling Triggers

Hair-Pulling Situations/Times:

- ☐ Living room
- ☐ Bedroom
- ☐ Bathroom
- ☐ Car
- ☐ Den
- ☐ Movie theater
- ☐ Classroom
- ☐ Evening after workday
- ☐ Morning in bed before arising
- ☐ Others _____

_____

_____

Hair-Pulling Activities:

- ☐ Reading
- ☐ Television
- ☐ Talking on the phone
- ☐ Putting children to bed
- ☐ Falling asleep in bed

- ☐ Using the computer
- ☐ Doing homework
- ☐ Doing paperwork/bills
- ☐ Taking a test
- ☐ Morning grooming
- ☐ Making decisions
- ☐ Using the toilet
- ☐ Others _____

_____

_____

Hair-Pulling Feelings:

- ☐ Sadness
- ☐ Worry
- ☐ Boredom
- ☐ Shame
- ☐ Fatigue
- ☐ Restlessness
- ☐ Irritability
- ☐ Fascination
- ☐ Excitement
- ☐ Guilt
- ☐ Others _____

_____

_____

Hair-Pulling Urges:

- ☐ To comfort
- ☐ To relieve
- ☐ To escape
- ☐ To fix or make perfect
- ☐ To eat

□ To express anger

□ To express self-hatred

□ Others _____

_____

_____

Hair-Pulling Sensations:

□ Tingly

□ Itchy

□ Sensitive

□ Painful

□ Pressure

□ Others _____

_____

_____

Hair-Pulling Thoughts:

□ What does one hair matter?

□ I can't concentrate without pulling this hair out first.

□ I might as well pull them all out so I can start over.

□ I'll start after I pull this one.

□ I deserve to pull out this hair.

□ I'm not able to cope without pulling.

□ If I don't pull this hair out it will bother me until I do.

□ I have a right to pull my hair out if I want to.

□ I need to pull these eyelashes out to make it look like the other side.

□ Others _____

_____

_____

Now that you have completed this list, you have a better picture of those variables that are involved with your hair-pulling profile.

Just by identifying these triggers, you should be more aware of them in the future. Greater awareness will help you plan in advance for "high risk" situations. It will be useful to remind yourself of these triggers on a frequent basis, as well as check to see if you have developed any new triggers for your habit. We suggest that you go over this list every couple of weeks to help prevent your hair pulling from becoming automatic once again.

Your awareness is necessary, though not sufficient, for you to become better equipped to manage your hair pulling. The next exercise will help you collect more data for cue identification so that you will be ready to design your own behavioral treatment plan.

Exercise: Self-Monitoring Hair Pulling and Associated Cues

You have already begun the task of outlining your individual hair-pulling cue profile. The following exercise will help you to identify some "hidden" triggers of which you may have been unaware. It is not unusual for hair pullers to be able to identify only a subset of their triggers until they actually self-monitor their pulling as it occurs.

Use the following self-monitoring record to document all instances of your hair pulling for the next week. Use a separate sheet for each day of the week (you'll want to make several photocopies before you begin). You will be asked to record many specifics of your habit including the time of day, situation, activity, emotion, thoughts, urge level, and number of hairs extracted. You should carry this log around with you and make your entries as soon as you can once you become aware of your hair pulling. This means even making an entry if you are in the midst of your habit!

Some hair-pulling episodes are easier to record, as they have definite beginnings and ends. Other episodes, however, may be less discrete and include off-and-on pulling over a span of hours. Do your best at deciding what you will define as an episode. We encourage you to label shorter rather than longer periods of hair pulling as episodes, as this will cause you to monitor more closely and increase your awareness even more. Some people find that their hair pulling occurs too often during the day to record each individual episode. If this is the case for you, try to initially record for specified time periods each day (e.g., Monday 7 A.M.–12 P.M., Tuesday 12 P.M.–5 P.M., etc.). As you get better and your hair pulling decreases, you will be able to monitor for longer stretches of time.

To help you better understand how to complete your self-monitoring log, we have included a record from a sample hair puller for your review. The completed log below lists the pulling episodes experienced by a forty-five-year-old professional sales woman during the first half of a normal workday. She often pulls in response to work stress, when experiencing a certain feeling in her upper eyelid, and when discovering hair that "doesn't belong." She reports a visual fascination with texture and color differences in her hair and finds it satisfying to play with the hair in her fingers and chew the hair root. She is not always immediately aware of pulling urges or the actual behavior until after she has already extracted hairs. She pulls from both her scalp and eyelashes and can identify a range in intensity of hair-pulling urges.

After you have recorded your hair pulling for an entire week, take a moment to analyze the data you have collected. First, count up the number of hairs you pulled each day. If you add the daily totals and divide by seven, you will have an average number of hairs pulled per day. Note: If your pulling is more binge-like than habitual, you may wish to just record the daily totals, since averaging may camouflage important variability in your hair-pulling habit.

For each remaining column on your monitoring sheet (except for the date), you want to identify subcategories and then tally how often these subcategories were recorded. For example, for time of day, you may wish to divide the day into hourly increments from the time you wake up in the morning to the time you retire at night (e.g., 7–8 A.M., 8–9 A.M., 9–10 A.M., etc.). For length of pulling episode, you may wish to use the following categories: less than one minute, one to five minutes, five to fifteen minutes, fifteen to thirty minutes, thirty minutes to one hour, and greater than one hour. (Depending on the pattern of your hair pulling, you may wish to select other subcategories that would better represent your unique hair-pulling pattern.) For body area, you can use the sites identified in the key at the bottom of your monitoring sheet. Once you have done this for every column, sit back and digest your results. This exercise is the most accurate and thorough way for you to identify the unique specifics of your hair-pulling habit. By completing this exercise, you have made tremendous strides in unraveling your hair-pulling problem.

You have now completed several exercises designed to assess the severity of your hair pulling and your signature hair-pulling pattern (including your unique triggers). Now let's discuss the potential role for significant others in the assessment of your hair-pulling behavior.

Sample Hair Pulling Self-Monitoring Log

Name: Harriet

Period: 8/13 to 8/19

Date	Time of Day	Length of Episode	# of Hairs Pulled and Body Area*	Rate Urge to Pull (0–10)	Situation and Activity	Describe Emotions, Thoughts, and Sensory Experiences	What Did You Do with the Hair After Pulling?	When Did You Notice the Hair Pulling? Why Did You Stop?
8/13	7:45 A.M.	15 secs.	2 s	3	Standing in front of closet deciding what to wear for an important meeting.	Felt anxious and ambivalent regarding clothes selection. Thinking about how to make the best impression at sales meeting.	Dropped hair on floor after biting off root and chewing.	Not aware until after extracted the hairs. Stopped pulling once became aware.
8/13	8:10 A.M.	3 mins.	8 el	8	Looking in bathroom mirror, applying eye makeup.	Still very anxious. Noticed one white el and felt that it "didn't belong." Pulled out several surrounding els inadvertently.	Visually examined extracted white el in the mirror. Stopped pulling after removed white el.	Aware of urge to pull el when observed it in the mirror. Stopped for differences in color and texture. Rolled el between fingers for several minutes.
8/13	9:40 A.M.	1 min.	4 el	7	Sitting at desk in office preparing morning presentation.	Distressed and upset after realizing error in slide. Obsessing about whether others will notice and what they will think. Felt a "tingling" sensation in right upper els.	Discarded hair once extracted as had no time to inspect it.	Became aware only after "tingling" feeling started. Stopped when interrupted by coworker and had to leave for meeting.
8/13	11:50 A.M.	10 mins.	23 s	5	Back in office after meeting was over, reviewing its outcome.	Felt depressed, guilty, and upset with self. Kept obsessing over how I should have checked the slides earlier and done more preparation.	Kept rubbing hair roots across lips, biting off the root and chewing into little bits.	Not fully aware until after had pulled several hairs. Felt like I was in a trance. Finally stopped when got upset with myself over my hair pulling and had to leave for lunch date.

*Key: s = scalp, eb = eyebrows, el = eyelashes, ch = chin, b = beard, p = pubis, l = legs, a = arm, o = other

Hair Pulling Self-Monitoring Log

Name: _____   Period: _____ to _____

Date	Time of Day	Length of Episode	# of Hairs Pulled and Body Area*	Rate Urge to Pull (0–10)	Situation and Activity	Describe Emotions, Thoughts, and Sensory Experiences	What Did You Do with the Hair After Pulling?	When Did You Notice the Hair Pulling? Why Did You Stop?

*Key: s = scalp, eb = eyebrows, el = eyelashes, ch = chin, b = beard, p = pubis, l = legs, a = arm. o=other

Source: B. O. Rothbaum, D. C. Opdyke, and N. J. Keuthen. 1999. In *Trichotillomania*, edited by D. J. Stein, G. A. Christenson, and E. Hollander. Washington, D.C.: American Psychiatric Press, Inc. Reprinted with permission.

Significant Others' Report of Hair Pulling

In general, the self-monitoring tools outlined so far in this chapter, in conjunction with the rating scale, are the best assessment measures for hair pulling. In some cases, however, there may be an additional value to seeking out the report of a significant other. Of course, many hair pullers are reluctant to do this for several reasons. Many have not disclosed their problem to others, in some cases not even to their partner or parents. Others prefer not to involve close family or friends in this process because of tension that has developed in the relationship due to the hair pulling. In still other cases, seeking feedback may shift the dynamic of the existing relationship in a direction that is unacceptable to the hair puller.

However, in some cases, particularly those in which the individual pulls hair without awareness, the report of a significant other may be useful. Accurate assessment requires an awareness that the behavior is occurring. Thus, if the hair puller ingests the hair, or disposes of it in a manner that it is not retrievable, he or she may be unable to provide an accurate tally of hair-pulling frequency. Also, in situations where individuals unconsciously stroke or play with their hair, not always resulting in hair pulling, significant others may provide a more accurate estimate of time spent in such related behaviors. Of course, this assumes that the pulling occurs in front of the significant other, and not only in privacy.

Feedback from a significant other may also be useful in those cases where the hair puller has an exaggerated perception of their hair loss. In some cases like this, the individual may have such exaggerated physical concerns that they could be diagnosed with *body dysmorphic disorder* (BDD). BDD is a condition in which one believes that he or she has a physical defect that is not real or exaggerates the severity of a slight physical problem. Thus, hair pullers might believe that the amount of their hair loss is much worse than it is in reality. In these cases, the global impression of significant others may provide a more accurate barometer of the extent of loss (if it is visible) than that of the hair pullers themselves. Alternatively, in cases where hair pullers are in denial of the severity of their problem, the significant other's report would also be a better assessment of the extent of hair loss than that of the hair puller's.

The Role of Stress in Symptom Worsening

One of the most difficult challenges is to identify those variables unique to the individual hair puller that explains his or her hair-pulling pattern. Each hair puller has his or her own "cue profile," which consists of the hair puller's unique configuration of hair-pulling triggers. This profile consists of common situations, thoughts, feeling states, and physical sensations that increase the likelihood that the individual will engage in hair pulling. Just as each individual has different common triggers, each hair puller can also have other life factors that worsen his or her hair pulling. Among these are situational stress and other psychological difficulties.

Stress is one of the most common events that can worsen an individual's hair pulling. By stress we mean the negative subjective experience of a certain event or situation. What is experienced as stressful by one hair puller is not necessarily experienced in the same fashion by another. For example, some individuals may find giving public speeches or visiting in-laws stressful. For other individuals, these events may be stimulating or relaxing.

Premenstrual symptoms are another commonly reported stressor that many women associate with the worsening of their hair pulling. One of the authors asked a large sample of female hair pullers to retrospectively rate the intensity of their hair-pulling symptoms for the weeks before, during, and after menstruation (Keuthen et al. 1997). Premenstrual worsening was reported for actual hair pulling, urge intensity and frequency, and the ability to control hair pulling. Hair-pulling symptom worsening was reduced during menstruation and shortly thereafter.

Each hair puller needs to be as specific as possible in behaviorally defining what stress consists of for them. Once you have identified the situation or experiences that you perceive as stressful, you will be more likely to recognize, anticipate, and plan for these events in the future. The next exercise will help you identify those events and situations that you find stressful so that you can use this information to minimize their impact on your hair pulling.

Exercise: Identifying Stressful Events

Below is a list of several events that other hair pullers have experienced as stressful. As mentioned earlier, it is important that you define what you experience as stressful. Check off those things you find stressful and add additional stressors in the blank spaces at the bottom of the list.

Checklist of Stressful Events

□ Upsetting phone calls

□ Visits with your parents or in-laws

□ Public speaking engagements

□ Physical illness

□ Increased workload

□ Arguments with your partner or children

□ Doing your taxes

□ Financial problems

□ Making important decisions

□ Premenstrual symptoms

□ Adverse weather conditions

□ Other _____

□ Other _____

□ Other _____

Other Psychological or Emotional Problems Associated with Hair-Pulling

Many accounts of trichotillomania in the scientific literature suggest that hair pulling can be accompanied by other psychological or emotional problems (e.g., depression, anxiety disorders, alcoholism, eating disorders, etc.). It is important to assess for this, as the presence of other problems may complicate treatment and negatively impact the outcome. Furthermore, specific evaluation for co-occurring problems is important since depression can often go undiagnosed and untreated. It is also not unusual for patients with panic disorder to not know that there is a name for the anxiety attacks that they experience.

In a longitudinal follow-up study conducted by one of the authors, those hair pullers with the most improvement in their hair pulling after treatment also had significant decreases in their levels of depression (Keuthen et al. 1998). Unfortunately, it is impossible to know which came first, improvement in mood or improvement in hair pulling. However, it suggests that it may be important to address some accompanying disorders, especially depression, to effectively treat hair pulling. It is not the case, however, that all hair pullers suffer from these problems. In fact, 10–20 percent of hair pullers do not have any other psychological disorders.

Before drawing any firm conclusions about the co-occurrence of other psychological or emotional problems, it is important to consider the sources of these observations. For example, it has been suggested that most reports of these problems in patients with trichotillomania appear in psychiatry journals. Alternatively, reports in dermatology and psychology journals usually identify hair pulling as an isolated symptom. This discrepancy may simply reflect the fact that psychiatrists are more likely to inquire about the presence of various emotional problems. Alternatively, one could also argue that hair pullers with no other problems are more prone to seek out a dermatologist or behavioral psychologist, while those with associated depression or severe anxiety are more likely to pursue care from a psychiatrist. While this hypothesis sounds plausible, our experience has not shown this to be the case. Since most people with trichotillomania don't know where to obtain services, they often seek out anyone with a reputation for offering hair-pulling services, regardless of their professional discipline.

What may be more important, though, are the characteristics of those hair pullers who never seek help. It is possible that these individuals, who may even represent the norm, have fewer additional problems or less severe hair pulling than those people that clinicians treat and researchers typically study.

Emotional and other mental health problems can be described in a number of different ways. One method is that outlined in the fourth edition of the *Diagnostic and Statistical Manual* (*DSM-IV*) of the American Psychiatric Association. In this system, clinical disorders are identified by groups of symptoms reported to be typical for the disorder. (In those cases where research is insufficient, the characteristic symptoms are determined by expert consensus.) Most research on groups of patients with trichotillomania has used instruments based on the definitions of disorders from the *DSM*. Thus, this literature tends to concentrate more on the presence or absence of clinical disorders (e.g., major depressive disorder) than on variability in a trait along a continuum (e.g., degree or extent of depression).

This distinction is important because more diagnostic-based research will not capture subclinical levels of emotional problems (e.g., depression or anxiety) in those pullers who do not satisfy full criteria for *DSM* diagnoses. For example, in one study approximately 25 percent of trichotillomania patients were diagnosed with generalized anxiety disorder given their extensive anxiety and worry. It is our impression, however, that some degree of anxiety plays a substantial role in a much larger proportion of hair pullers. It is likely the case that they simply fail to describe all the necessary symptoms to have it called an actual disorder.

With all of this in mind, let's look at the results from a study of nearly two hundred trichotillomania patients in the clinic of one of the authors (DJS). The most common emotional problem accompanying trichotillomania was reported to be depression. About one-half of hair pullers seen in clinical situations either report an episode of significant depression at some point in their lives or a history of chronic depression. About one-third of patients are experiencing this depression at the time that they present for evaluation. This is much higher than one would expect in the general population, suggesting that trichotillomania has some association with mood problems.

Several different depression diagnoses are found in *DSM-IV*. Major depressive disorder refers to one or more episodes of depression during which the individual experiences either depressed mood or loss of interest or pleasure for at least a two-week period. During this time it is also required that the individual has at least four other symptoms including weight loss; sleep changes; psychomotor agitation or retardation; fatigue or loss of energy; feelings of worthlessness or guilt; concentration problems or indecisiveness; or suicidal ideation, plan, or attempt. Dysthymia refers to a more chronic depression lasting for at least two years and accompanied by two other symptoms (but not meeting criteria for a major depressive disorder). An adjustment disorder with depression refers to the onset of depressed mood within a three-month period after the occurrence of a significant stressor. The depression is felt to be excessive given the nature of the stress and results in significant functional impairment. Depressive disorder not otherwise specified refers to depressive symptoms that do not meet criteria for any of the disorders described above.

What is not clear to us is the direction of the relationship between depression and hair pulling. In other words, how often are mood problems a result of the experience of hair pulling? Or, alternatively, does depression bring out hair pulling? Another possibility would be that there is something about certain people that makes them vulnerable to develop both problems. The same can be said, of course, for other emotional conditions known to occur frequently in hair pullers. Given that a relationship between depression and hair pulling has often been reported, we recommend that you assess the extent to which you may be depressed. If you are unsure, you may wish to seek professional consultation to help you.

Anxiety disorders are also frequently detected in people who present for treatment of trichotillomania. Over a quarter of these patients are diagnosed with generalized anxiety disorder, a condition characterized by persistent multiple worries and accompanying physical symptoms (e.g., restlessness, being easily fatigued, poor concentration, muscle tension, poor sleep, etc.). Ten percent of hair pullers have had frequent panic attacks. These are brief surges of anxiety accompanied by a sense of loss of control, impending doom, or fear of dying. Individuals with panic attacks also experience physical symptoms (e.g., shortness of breath, racing or pounding heart, dizziness or light-headedness, sweating, tingling in hands or around the mouth, trembling, a sense of choking, and/or the experience of flushing). Discomfort in social situations also occurs in about 10 percent of hair pullers. The main themes here are a persistent fear of embarrassing oneself when speaking, eating, or engaging in other social activities, or a general concern about others always scrutinizing one's actions. A history of other specific fears, such as heights or animals, is common, but these fears have generally resolved by the time the patient presents for hair-pulling treatment.

One of the most interesting findings is the large proportion of hair pullers who have (or did have) obsessive-compulsive disorder (OCD). OCD is an anxiety disorder characterized by obsessions and compulsions (see the introduction to this book). Around 15 percent of people with hair pulling also suffer from OCD. Some studies actually report even higher rates than this. In contrast, only about 2 percent of the general population suffer from OCD. This finding supports the hypothesis of some investigators that trichotillomania and OCD have an important relationship with each other. We will return to this interesting idea in chapter 3.

Lastly, hair pulling may be associated more commonly than expected with eating disorders (e.g., bulimia) and substance abuse. Additionally, there probably is a higher likelihood of hair pulling in developmentally delayed and disabled individuals and patients with chronic, severe, mental disorders (such as schizophrenia) than in the general population. Unfortunately, though, little systematic research has been conducted with these populations.

In conclusion, numerous reports document associations between hair pulling and other disturbances of mood, thought, or behavior. If your hair pulling occurs along with other problems, you may choose to seek help from a mental health professional. They would have the expertise to appropriately diagnose any additional problems and to help you locate appropriate treatment for these disorders. However, as stated earlier, one-tenth to one-fifth of hair pullers have no reported history of another mental disorder. Thus, hair pulling does not necessarily predict the presence of another psychiatric condition.

Family History of Hair Pulling

Little research has been done to date investigating the family history of hair pulling in individuals with this problem. The data that does exist generally reports about a 5 percent incidence of this disorder in first-degree relatives (e.g., parents, siblings, or children) of hair pullers. One can question the validity of this data as it requires relatives to be honest in their report of hair-pulling symptoms. It is unlikely that older relatives would have historically been given a diagnosis of trichotillomania since little attention was paid to this disorder until recently. Furthermore, in days gone by, older relatives would have had an easier time hiding these symptoms given that the use of wigs, false eyelashes, eyebrow pencil, and other cosmetics were very much in vogue.

It is difficult to know how to interpret the evidence for the increased incidence of trichotillomania documented in close relatives. We cannot conclude from this finding alone that genetics are involved in its etiology. It is also conceivable that *observational modeling* accounts for this finding. In other words, individuals can develop hair pulling merely by mimicking the behavior that they observe in their close relatives. Definitive answers regarding the role of familial factors in the development of trichotillomania awaits future research.

Impact on Social Relationships

In almost all cases, hair pulling has a significant impact on interpersonal relationships. In more minor cases, individuals may avoid certain activities with others out of fear that their hair pulling may be revealed. Among these activities are athletic endeavors, going to the beach, being out in inclement weather, and sitting in the orchestra level of a theater. In more extreme cases, hair pullers may avoid intimacy and may even choose their profession on the basis of the amount of public exposure involved in their job.

It is often the case that significant tension and conflict develop in more intimate relationships as a result of the hair pulling. Hair pullers may fear exposure and withdraw to hide their hair-pulling behavior or camouflage its results. The hair puller may be late for engagements when caught in a hair-pulling binge or when attempting to hide the physical damage. It's not unusual for hair pullers to offer alternative explanations for hair loss and consequently feel deceptive and dishonest in their relationships. The family member or friend may sense a change in the hair puller's behavior when he or she is experiencing difficulties controlling symptoms, but loved ones may still be unable to identify what is happening. As a result, they may erroneously conclude that the hair puller is upset with them or rejecting them. In those situations where a significant other is critical or intolerant of the behavior, the hair puller can suffer from lowered self-esteem. Family and friends may feel helpless in dealing with the problem and, on occasion, resort to ineffective methods in an effort to thwart further hair loss. The following case study illustrates how hair pulling may negatively impact relationships in many different ways.

Betsy is a thirty-two-year-old single, female author who recalls pulling out her scalp hair since her early teen years. She can vividly recall writing one of her first short stories and being shocked by the amount of hair on the floor around her desk when finished. Betsy was able to keep her secret from her parents and siblings for several years as her hair loss was easily camouflaged by alternative hair styles. Her mother would always nag her to wear her hair down so that she "would look more feminine." When Betsy insisted on wearing her hair in a ponytail, her mother assumed that it was an adolescent fad and she was merely asserting her independence.

Her sister and several of her friends were puzzled by the fact that she didn't want to participate in styling each other's hair and doing each other's makeup. Initially, they questioned whether she enjoyed spending time with them. On the other hand, she seemed eager to do other activities with them. But she was always so insistent on not going into the water at the beach, even on the hottest days of summer. Alternatively, they wondered if she just felt insecure about her looks and thought she didn't look attractive when her hair was wet.

As the years passed, Betsy's hair got thinner and thinner on the crown of her scalp. In her early twenties, she purchased a hair piece out of fear that she would be "found out" as the hair thinning became more visible. She was pleasantly surprised when she started getting compliments on her hair once she started to wear the piece. As a result of the positive attention, she started to feel more confident and outgoing. She found herself being asked out on dates to which, for the most part, she had no regrets saying no. However, there came a time when she realized she was developing a strong attraction for a male coworker, Ben, who was showering her with more and more attention. For the first time in her life, she did not want to miss the opportunity to get to know a person better. So, when Ben asked her out, she readily agreed.

Betsy found herself anxious in anticipation of their first date, fearing that he might touch her hair and inadvertently discover one of the clips attaching the piece to her hair. While Ben was aware that she seemed anxious their first time out together, he decided that she was just initially uncomfortable until she got to know someone better. Several dates later, though, he began to question why she recoiled every time he tried to stroke her hair. He also began to notice over time that she avoided certain activities including bike riding, swimming, and going for walks in windy or rainy weather. He became increasingly confused, as this behavior seemed inconsistent with her expression of fond feelings for him.

Realizing that Ben was becoming more and more confused by her behavior, Betsy decided that she needed to confide in him. He immediately responded that of course he understood, given his nail-biting problems as a child. Before she could relate more details about her hair pulling, he told her that she could surely stop if she only "set her mind to it." With this, Betsy started to feel that the future of their relationship depended on her ability to control her problem.

Ben started to make comments on how striking other women's hair was, believing this would serve as an incentive for her to exhibit more control. When Betsy soon after had a bad bout of hair pulling, her self-esteem plummeted. She became fearful that he would ask her how she was doing with her hair pulling. More and more, she found herself making excuses to get out of dates when she had undergone a recent pulling binge. It was only several weeks later that Ben announced he was breaking up with her, as he felt she no longer was interested in seeing him.

Identification of the interpersonal consequences resulting from the hair pulling is important for many reasons. Identifying negative outcomes is likely to enhance the hair puller's motivation to tackle the problem. In other cases, it may underscore the need for couples counseling to resolve some of the relationship conflicts that have contributed to stress. Goals for couples counseling may include educational interventions for the significant other, discussion of communication patterns focusing on the hair pulling, and problem-solving useful and supportive roles for the hair puller's partner. The exercise below will help you to identify specific roles for family and friends to assist you in your treatment efforts. Additional guidance for families and friends will be presented later on in chapter 9.

Exercise: Identifying Roles for Significant Others

Following is a checklist for you to complete by answering "yes" or "no" to each question.

	Yes	No
Would you like your family and friends to learn more about trichotillomania?	____	____
If yes, how? Reading	____	____
Discussion	____	____
Conference/Lecture	____	____
Other _____		
Would you like them to ask you how you are doing?	____	____
If yes, how often? Daily	____	____
Weekly	____	____
Monthly	____	____
Other _____		
Would you like others to signal you when you are touching or pulling?	____	____
If yes, how? Verbally	____	____
Physical prompt	____	____
Other _____		

	Yes	No

Would you like others to positively comment if
they notice regrowth?   ____   ____

    If yes, suggest how you would like them to say it:

_____

_____

Would you like others to comment if they notice
hair thinning or bald patches?   ____   ____

    If yes, suggest how you would like them to say it:

_____

_____

Would you like them to distract you or suggest an
alternative activity if they notice you are pulling?   ____   ____

Would you like them to suggest coping tools if they
notice you are having a difficult time?   ____   ____

    If yes, what?   Hand toys   ____   ____

                             Barrier methods
                             (e.g., hat/gloves)   ____   ____

                             Change activities   ____   ____

                             Other _____

Would you like them to stay in physical proximity
to you during difficult times?   ____   ____

    If yes, when?   Television   ____   ____

                             Reading   ____   ____

                             Computer   ____   ____

                             Bathroom   ____   ____

                             Other _____

Would you like them to massage your hands or
scalp if you have urges or feel stressed?   ____   ____

Would you like them to ask how you are doing if
you appear stressed in general?   ____   ____

Please specify other ways your family and friends can help you control your pulling or show emotional support:

_____

_____

_____

_____

Note: This is the last exercise for this chapter. Chapters 3 and 4 are informational and do not include exercises. Read them while you practice hair-pulling self-monitoring and other exercises discussed thus far. Exercises resume in chapter 5.

Summary Points

➤ A complete hair-pulling evaluation should assess the severity of hair pulling, triggers for the behavior, family history of hair pulling, co-occurring psychological problems, and impact on social relationships.

➤ Individualized assessment of hair-pulling behavior and triggers is critical for development of the most effective self-help program.

➤ Assessment of hair pulling should occur before, during, and after treatment efforts.

➤ Multiple methods of assessment, such as self-monitoring and the use of a rating scale, should be used whenever possible.

➤ Assessment alone often reduces the occurrence of hair pulling through the phenomenon of *behavioral reactivity*.

Chapter 3

What Causes Hair Pulling?

In this chapter we will explore the various causes of hair pulling. Many different theories have been put forward to explain this problem. These range from the neurobiological (e.g., involving brain regions, brain chemicals, or inherited genes) to the psychological (e.g., involving underlying mental conflicts, stressful events, or family interactions). It is likely that different factors contribute to this problem in different people.

Stress and Hair Pulling

Many of our patients believe that their hair pulling is caused by stress.

Jenny, one of our patients, sought help just before she was scheduled to take her state bar examination. A few weeks earlier she had started to pull out her hair. As the exam drew closer, the bald spot on the crown of her scalp had grown larger and larger. She had pulled out her hair in the weeks before writing other exams, but the bar exam was her most important professional hurdle. Now her hair pulling was out of control.

For Jenny, her hair pulling was clearly stress-related. She was convinced that as soon as the exam was over and her vacation started, she would only have occasional urges to pull her hair. She worried a lot, though, about beginning a stressful legal career. She feared that the continuous deadlines and nonstop working hours might result in her pulling out all of her hair and going bald. It was this thought that finally led her to seek professional help.

Many other hair pullers, however, are convinced that stress plays no role whatsoever in their problem.

Marge was a sixty-one-year-old civil engineer when she first sought help. During a highly successful business career, she had risen through the ranks of a large construction company to become managing director. The enormous stresses of her job had been compounded, she felt, by the difficulties of being a woman in a traditionally male field. She had always worked doubly hard to prove that she deserved to be where she was. She had regarded her hair pulling as a side effect of this stress and was sure that it would disappear after she retired at age sixty. But, to her dismay, it didn't.

For Marge, it was now clear that her hair pulling was not stress-related. Thinking about the previous years more carefully, she noted that the hair pulling had waxed and waned in intensity with no clear relationship to changes in the stress level in her life. Furthermore, her hair pulling was always triggered in situations in which she was relaxed. These included taking a late night bath or watching a favorite sitcom on television after a long day's work. Now that she had been retired for a year, spending increasing amounts of time under no particular pressure at all, her hair pulling was worse than ever.

Our earlier discussion of hair-pulling cues confirms the views held by both Jenny and Marge. For many people with hair pulling, stress results in increased urges. For many others, however, hair pulling is associated with sedentary activities or relaxed situations. Some people state that their hair pulling is worse during times of stress, while others notice hair pulling during times of relaxation. In summary, while stress can make hair pulling worse, this is by no means universally true for everyone with hair pulling.

Hair Pulling and Symbolic Meanings

For much of this century, the views of Freud and his followers have strongly influenced mental health professionals. Only a few decades ago, most leaders in the field of psychiatry were psychoanalysts who had completed their residency training in psychiatry and had pursued additional studies in the theories and practices of Freud and others.

Thus, many of the first articles on trichotillomania, which were written earlier this century, demonstrated a strong psychoanalytic influence. These authors often focused on the unconscious meaning of hair pulling. After all, the central tenets of psychoanalytic theory are that all of our behaviors are influenced by the unconscious. In fact, even seemingly irrational behaviors were believed to make sense when we could understand their unconscious meaning.

Many different symbolic meanings have been put forward for hair pulling. Since hair may represent strength and virility, the extraction of hair may represent a loss of power or castration. Alternatively, hair may signify physical beauty and seduction. (One example of this is Rapunzel, who gave her lover access to her tower by lowering her tresses.) Thus, pulling out one's hair may represent a denial of sexuality or a loss of love. Caroline Koblenzer (1987), a dermatologist and psychoanalyst, concludes that hair may be used symbolically to represent conflicts around a variety of sexual issues in both men and women.

Although psychoanalytic explanations of hair pulling sometimes seem elegant, they are often problematic. Most importantly, there is little empirical evidence that actually supports them. Not only is there no research that actually shows a link between hair pulling and unconscious meaning, but there are no treatment studies that demonstrate the therapeutic value of psychoanalytic interpretations of hair pulling. Psychoanalytically oriented psychotherapy may have some role in helping sufferers, though likely not by directly impacting the hair pulling itself. (For a further discussion of psychoanalytic treatment and its outcome for hair pulling, see chapter 5.)

Parents and Children

Psychoanalytic theory has developed and changed over the years. While early psychoanalysts emphasized the importance of unconscious wishes, later psychoanalytic thinking focused on the importance of relationships for the understanding of people and their problems. For example, this latter perspective proposed that difficulties in early mother-infant bonding may be at the root of later difficulties in intimacy, as well as explain distorted ways of seeing oneself and others.

Similarly, other psychoanalytically-oriented authors have examined early mother-daughter relationships in order to explain the later development of hair pulling. It has been suggested that hair pulling emerges in the context of troubled mother-daughter relationships in which both hostility and overprotection are simultaneously present (Greenberg and Sarner 1965). They also reported that hair pulling occurred subsequent to the actual or threatened loss of this relationship.

Once again, there has been little hard research to confirm such a point of view. Researchers who study related disorders also characterized by repetitive symptoms, such as obsessive-compulsive disorder (OCD) and Tourette's disorder (TD) previously known as Tourette's Syndrome, have not found that these disorders can be traced to family difficulties. If anything, the finding that both OCD and TD tend to run in families has strengthened biological hypotheses that propose an important hereditary or genetic component.

Now and again, however, clinicians also see women with hair pulling who have suffered tremendous abuse during their childhood. An example of this scenario is Cathy, who presented for treatment after she had pulled out all of her scalp and pubic hair. She noted that she often felt confused and that her emotions vacillated between anger, rage, hurt, and sadness. There also had been times when she abused alcohol and had difficulty in forming stable relationships with men. She admitted that between the ages of twelve and eighteen years old her alcoholic father had repeatedly molested her.

For Cathy, hair pulling was one of a number of symptoms that she traced back to her traumatic childhood years. It is not unusual for hair pulling and other self-injurious behaviors to occur in survivors of incest and other kinds of abuse. In these individuals self-injurious behavior may be triggered by situations or emotions (such as feeling abandoned) that are reminiscent of past traumas. A long-term and intensive psychotherapy, in which past and current relationships are closely examined, may often be necessary in these cases to allow deep healing to take place.

On the other hand, it has been our experience that many people with hair pulling recall wonderfully carefree and happy childhood years. Similarly, many people with hair pulling describe their current relationships as not particularly problematic and are unable to link their hair pulling with relationship issues. Thus, a history of difficult or abusive relationships is another factor that may be important in some hair pullers, but which is definitely not a universal feature of the disorder.

Family History of Hair Pulling

It has long been known that many medical and psychiatric disorders run in families. The development of modern genetics has led to an understanding of the precise ways in which these disorders can be inherited. Each of us inherits hundreds of thousands of pairs of genes from our parents, with one set each from our mothers and fathers. These genes consist of a chemical called deoxyribonucleic acid (DNA), which has been called "the molecule of life." It is ultimately responsible for all the chemical processes in our body, as it provides a blueprint for the production of the proteins that make up our cells.

Some medical disorders can be traced to a single pair of faulty genes. For example, in the blood disorder known as sickle cell anemia, a tiny aberration in one pair of genes leads to the production of abnormal hemoglobin (the protein responsible for carrying oxygen in the red cells of our blood). If only one of the pair of genes is defective (e.g., the gene inherited from the father is normal, but the gene inherited from the mother is abnormal), then the person does not manifest the illness but is known as "a carrier." It is only when two carriers have a child, and when that child receives the faulty gene from both parents, that the disease will manifest itself.

The genetic transmission of many other medical disorders, however, is much more complicated. Diabetes and hypertension are two illnesses that illustrate this point. Although they both have an important genetic component, several different sets of genes play a role and environmental factors may also be important in triggering the illness. Thus, in these disorders, it seems that particular combinations of genes result in a predisposition to manifest the illness under particular kinds of environmental circumstances. Psychiatric disorders in which genetic inheritance plays an important role (e.g., OCD and TD) are also likely to involve several different sets of genes that lead to a predisposition to develop the disorder under certain conditions.

One way to determine the extent to which a disorder is genetically influenced is through family studies. A good test of the role of genetic variables is to see whether identical twins (who inherit exactly the same DNA) raised in different environments have the same disorders. Unfortunately, this kind of study has yet to be done for hair pulling. However, a family study by researchers at the National Institute for Mental Health showed that hair pulling is more common in the families of people with trichotillomania than might be expected by chance alone (Lenane et al. 1992). This suggests that genetic factors may well contribute to hair pulling.

In summary, trichotillomania is not simply caused by one abnormal gene that is transmitted from parent to child. It is possible that several different sets of genes may play a role in predisposing people to develop hair-pulling tendencies. Tremendous progress is currently being made in understanding how genes operate to influence human behavior. In future years, researchers may well be able to identify the different genes that contribute to disorders like hair pulling. Through better understanding of the proteins manufactured by these genes, they may be able to identify the precise chemical processes in the brain that are responsible for these symptoms.

Serotonin and Other Brain Chemicals

The brain is made up of billions of individual nerve cells or neurons. These neurons communicate with one another by means of specific chemicals called *neurotransmitters*. While there are many different neurotransmitters, one called *serotonin* is particularly important in OCD, and perhaps also in hair pulling. (As noted earlier, research in trichotillomania has shown that this disorder is similar, but not identical, to OCD.) Other important neurotransmitters in the brain include dopamine and noradrenaline.

It first became clear that serotonin might play an important part in OCD when it was discovered that a medication called clomipramine was effective for this condition. Clomipramine is also used in the treatment of depression. However, clomipramine works mainly on the serotonin system, unlike other common antidepressants that were used at that time that affect both serotonin and noradrenaline.

The "serotonin hypothesis" of OCD gained further support when researchers conducted a well-designed study comparing clomipramine with desipramine in the treatment of OCD (Leonard et al. 1988). Importantly, desipramine, another antidepressant, primarily works on the noradrenergic neurotransmitter system. In contrast, clomipramine works primarily on the serotonin system. Clomipramine (whose trade name is Anafranil) proved to be far more effective in the treatment of OCD than desipramine. Furthermore, we now know that an entire group of drugs called selective serotonin reuptake inhibitors (or SSRIs) are all effective in the treatment of OCD. These act even more specifically on the serotonin system than clomipramine. (See table 3.1 for a list of the available SSRI medications.)

TABLE 3.1:
List of available selective serotonin reuptake inhibitors (SSRIs)

Chemical Name	Trade Name
Citalopram	Celexa, Cipramil
Fluoxetine	Prozac
Fluvoxamine	Luvox
Paroxetine	Paxil, Arapax
Sertraline	Zoloft

It is a possibility that other neurotransmitters are also involved in OCD. Many patients with OCD also suffer from tics, which are involuntary movements or vocalizations. For individuals with tics, the dopamine neurotransmitter system appears to play a particularly important role. Psychiatrists have learned that when treating people who suffer from both OCD and tics, it may be useful to combine a SSRI with a medication that works on the dopamine system.

An early hypothesis proposed that serotonin could also be important in trichotillomania given the possible links between OCD and hair pulling discussed in the introduction of this book. Following up on earlier research that showed clomipramine to be more effective than desipramine in children with OCD, Swedo, Leonard, et al. (1989) decided to compare these two medications in people with hair pulling. In this early landmark study, they found that clomipramine was superior to desipramine in the treatment of trichotillomania. Furthermore, the beneficial response to clomipramine was maintained over many months.

Unfortunately, the outcomes of subsequent investigations of SSRI medications in the treatment of hair pulling have not been as clear cut. We will discuss these results in more depth in the following chapter on medication treatment. For now, however, we note simply that the SSRIs are not always effective in reducing hair pulling. Furthermore, even when there is an early response to an SSRI, there may be a return to baseline hair-pulling levels over the next several months. These findings shed doubt on the hypothesis that serotonin alone is involved in the problem of hair pulling and on the hypothesis that trichotillomania and OCD are identical disorders.

Perhaps it is the case that serotonin plays a role in hair pulling in combination with other neurotransmitters. One question that researchers have been interested in is whether patients with hair pulling, like patients with OCD and tics, would respond to the combination of SSRIs with other agents that work on the dopamine system. There has been relatively little research on this question. Nevertheless, some data does exist to suggest that some people with hair pulling do, in fact, respond to this combination of medications. We will discuss this research in greater detail in the next chapter.

The human brain is highly complex, and it is likely that other chemicals are also involved in hair pulling. Along these lines, the opioid system is of interest, as it has been shown to be involved in various kinds of self-mutilation. Opioids and opiates (like heroin) are pleasure- inducing drugs, and certain kinds of opioids may be released in the brain when the body is in pain. Therefore, one theory is that people with repetitive self-mutilation are addicted to the internal release of opioids by the brain. It turns out that a drug called naltrexone, which acts on the opioid system, may be effective in some people with trichotillomania (Christenson et al. 1994). This study will be reviewed in more detail in the next chapter.

Another neurochemical system that may be involved in hair pulling is the hormonal system. Male and female hormones are chemicals that affect other chemical processes throughout the body, including those of the brain. The fact that trichotillomania is more common in women may point to the involvement of the female hormonal system in hair pulling. In addition, hair pulling sometimes begins or is worsened during adolescence or during the premenstrual period, times when there are important hormonal changes.

In summary, it seems unlikely that hair pulling involves only one brain chemical. Instead, a number of brain chemical systems, including the serotonin, dopamine, opioid, and hormonal systems, may play a role. Much of this work is, however, only preliminary. Over the next few decades we can expect further research and a better understanding of the ways in which the neurochemicals of the brain influence hair pulling.

The Basal Ganglia and Grooming Disorders

Where exactly in the brain is the serotonin neurotransmitter system? As it turns out, serotonin can be found in most parts of the brain.

Nevertheless, serotonin neurons may be particularly important in those brain regions where there are increased amounts of the neurotransmitter. One such area is a circuit that runs from areas in the front of the brain (the *frontal lobes*) to a region of the brain called the *basal ganglia*. This circuit is of particular interest because there is growing evidence that it is important in producing the symptoms of OCD.

The development of new brain imaging technologies, which allow us to picture brain activity levels, have been particularly useful in this kind of research. In people with OCD, for example, research has shown marked hyperactivity in frontal-basal ganglia pathways. This increase in activity can be seen when an OCD sufferer is scanned in a relaxed state, but is brought out even further if the person is scanned when symptoms are activated (e.g., by bringing dirt into the room of an OCD patient with contamination obsessions).

Some of the most interesting research in this field has involved scanning the brains of people with OCD before and after treatment. Remarkably, successful treatment leads to a normalization of activity in frontal-basal ganglia pathways. Furthermore, it turns out that this normalization of brain activity can be achieved by using either anti-OCD medications or by employing certain kinds of psychotherapy, such as cognitive behavioral therapy. This exciting research suggests that the underlying "false alarm" that causes OCD can be switched off by either medications or behavioral changes.

Why is increased activity in the frontal-basal ganglia pathways important in OCD? One answer is that this brain area seems to be involved in executing inherited motor programs. For example, nest building in birds, food hoarding in rodents, and social grooming in monkeys are all complex motor programs that are innate and may involve the basal ganglia. One possibility is that excessive washing in humans is a form of "grooming disorder." In this scenario, evolved motor programs, which usually lie dormant in humans, are released. This abnormal release of these motor programs may itself reflect some sort of damage to the basal ganglia.

Are there similar sorts of brain changes in trichotillomania as in OCD? Unfortunately, there has been too little work to answer this question definitively. One study indicated that people with OCD and trichotillomania have different patterns of brain activity at rest (Swedo et al. 1991). However, those who responded to clomipramine had similar kinds of activity in a part of the frontal-basal ganglia circuit. Another study recently found that individuals with hair pulling may have smaller putamens, a small area in the brain that is part of the basal ganglia (O'Sullivan et al. 1997).

Thus, there is some data to suggest that while people with OCD and hair pulling have different patterns of brain activity, there may be involvement of the frontal-basal ganglia pathways in both hair pulling and OCD. It is possible to speculate that both OCD and hair pulling are "grooming disorders." In these disorders, damage to the basal ganglia leads to the abnormal release of motor programs (such as washing and hair pulling). Fortunately, both medication and behavioral therapies may be able to normalize basal ganglia function.

Streptococcal Infection and Hair Pulling

Occasionally, differences in the basal ganglia among individuals can be the result of direct damage to this area of the brain. If there is damage to the basal ganglia in OCD and hair pulling, then what could cause this damage? The answer to this question remains unknown. One of the most exciting areas of research addresses the possible role of infection in basal ganglia damage. In particular, researchers have been looking at the role played by a common throat infection, caused by a "bug" (or *bacterium*) known as streptococcus.

Ordinarily, streptococcus throat infections lead to nothing more than a few days of coughing and soreness. Every now and again, however, a serious complication known as rheumatic fever develops. Patients with rheumatic fever may develop serious heart or neurological conditions. The neurological condition is called Sydenham's chorea or St. Vitus' dance. It involves damage to the basal ganglia and is characterized by involuntary movements of various parts of the body.

Why does streptococcus throat infection usually lead to complete recovery, but occasionally result in rheumatic heart disease or Sydenham's chorea? When the body is attacked by bacteria, the immune system of the body produces antibodies, which are substances that try to destroy the foreign invader. Ordinarily, the antibodies do their job successfully, and the infection resolves without further complications.

Occasionally, however, the antibodies mistakenly also attack parts of the person's own body or brain. This phenomenon is known as autoimmunity. Unfortunately, some parts of the body and brain look similar to the outer wall of the streptococcus bacterium, so that there is room for possible error. When antibodies damage the basal ganglia, Sydenham's chorea results. As there are important genetic predispositions to the development of autoimmune processes, this theory also fits with the data mentioned earlier that genetic factors contribute to the development of hair pulling.

It turns out that people with Sydenham's chorea not only display involuntary movements, but they also may have behavioral problems. The famous physician William Osler noted, for example, that patients with Sydenham's chorea may have compulsions. Swedo, Rapoport, et al. (1989) decided to examine this association in more detail. They confirmed that there was a high incidence of OCD in those patients with Sydenham's chorea. As a result they began to study whether streptococcus infection could worsen cases of OCD and even hair pulling.

They found that in some cases of OCD and hair pulling, this is precisely what happens. Soon after suffering from a streptococcus throat infection, some patients show an exacerbation of OCD or hair pulling symptoms. In addition, there is now a report of a patient with Sydenham's chorea and hair pulling (Stein et al. 1997). This research suggests that autoimmune responses after streptococcal infection may play an important role in some cases of OCD and hair pulling. One might speculate that future treatment of these patients may even involve medications that act primarily on the immune system.

Summary Points

▶ Hair pulling may be attributed to different factors in different sufferers. Stress, unconscious conflict, and relationship difficulties may be important in some hair pullers, but are not universally present.

▶ The role of neurobiological factors remains under active investigation. Several different brain chemical systems may well play a role, including the dopamine, serotonin, opioid, and hormonal systems. The region of the brain known as the basal ganglia may also be important.

▶ One of the most exciting areas of research suggests that OCD and hair pulling may sometimes be worsened by autoimmune processes after streptococcus throat infection. This work could possibly lead to new avenues of treatment in the future.

➤ Several sets of genes may be involved in predisposing people to develop trichotillomania. It is possible, for example, that these genes are involved in the predisposition to autoimmune reactions, which then lead to hair pulling after streptococcus throat infection. Much research is needed, however, to move this argument beyond mere speculation.

Chapter 4

Medications for
Hair Pulling

In this chapter we will discuss the different medications that have been used in the treatment of trichotillomania. Until recently, psychiatrists rarely paid serious attention to the question of whether medications might help decrease hair pulling. Now, however, there are several promising developments in the use of medications for this problem. We will cover the pros and cons of such agents and provide some guidelines to help you answer the question of whether a particular individual with hair pulling should be on medication.

The Serotonin Reuptake Inhibitors

The first medications that were studied rigorously for the treatment of hair pulling were the serotonin reuptake inhibitors. This includes clomipramine and those drugs called the selective serotonin reuptake inhibitors (SSRIs). The SSRIs more specifically act on the serotonin system than clominpramine, though they all are classified as serotonin reuptake inhibitors. In the last chapter we discussed how these agents are currently the medication treatment of choice for people with obsessive-compulsive disorder (OCD). It was this finding that led to the "serotonin hypothesis" of OCD and that later led researchers to try these medications for the treatment of hair pulling. The serotonin hypothesis proposes that obsessive-compulsive behaviors result from dysregulation (often simplistically called a "chemical imbalance") of brain systems involving the neurotransmitter serotonin. (Neurotransmitters are chemicals that act as messengers between brain cells.)

Historically, before the advent of the SSRIs, the tricyclic antidepressants were the class of medications generally used to treat people with depression. Both clomipramine and desipramine are tricyclic antidepressants. While clomipramine (trade name is Anafranil) has serotonin in reuptake inhibitory properties, desipramine is primarily a noradrenergic reuptake inhibitor. (The term noradrenergic refers to noradrenaline, which is another brain messenger.) As reported in the previous chapter, Susan Swedo and her colleagues at the National Institute of Mental Health first demonstrated that clomipramine was more effective than desipramine for children with OCD, and then compared these same medications in adult hair pullers.

Swedo, Leonard, et al. (1989) published their exciting findings for hair pulling in the highly influential *New England Journal of Medicine*. Their article indicated that clomipramine was far more effective than desipramine in the short-term treatment of trichotillomania. (It should be emphasized here that even though the tricyclics are known as "antidepressants," clomipramine is effective for OCD and hair pulling whether or not depression is present.) Furthermore, in a subsequent paper, Swedo and her group (1993) reported that the positive response to clomipramine was maintained for many months in the majority of their hair-pulling patients.

It has largely been only in the last decade that the SSRIs have become available. These medications act exclusively on the serotonin system, while the tricyclic drugs affect both the serotonin and noradrenergic systems. Given their usefulness in the treatment of OCD, the obvious next question was whether the SSRIs would effectively treat trichotillomania.

Several studies have tried to answer this question. In some studies, the SSRIs were shown to reduce hair pulling. Unfortunately, in other studies they were shown to be ineffective. Furthermore, it has been noted that some patients who initially respond to treatment with a SSRI may relapse over the next several months despite ongoing treatment. Perhaps the best way of summarizing these conflicting studies is to say that while some hair pullers respond to the SSRIs, many others do not.

Is there any one serotonin reuptake inhibitor that is the best for hair pulling? To date, this question has not been well studied. However, it seems to be the case that some patients with either OCD or hair pulling can respond to one SSRI and not to another. Thus, if you do decide to use these medications to help reduce your hair pulling, we strongly suggest that if the first agent turns out to be ineffective, a second, and even a third, agent is tried.

Given the evidence for the effectiveness of clomipramine, it is reasonable to try this medication first, or, alternatively, when one or more of the SSRIs have proven ineffective. Given that hair pulling is likely to involve more than one neurotransmitter system, it is possible that clomipramine, which acts on several systems, is more effective than the SSRIs, which act primarily on a single system. On the other hand, since the SSRIs often have fewer side effects than clomipramine, many people with OCD or hair pulling choose to begin a medication treatment with one of the SSRI agents.

Sharon was a twenty-eight-year-old woman who had pulled out scalp hair since age fourteen. When she was sixteen years old, her parents insisted that she see a therapist to deal with an expanding bald spot that was becoming more difficult to hide. Inexperienced in treating trichotillomania, her therapist focused on family issues without specifically addressing aspects of the hair pulling itself. Sharon subsequently dropped out of therapy after a few months without any notable progress. For many years after, she just disguised her hair loss and avoided discussions about her hair pulling with her parents.

Her hair pulling continued on a nearly daily basis with exacerbations several times a year associated with stressful life events. Sharon finished college and was now near completion of a graduate degree. Recent stresses associated with her research appeared to worsen her hair pulling. Sharon had also been dating a man for three years. He was aware and accepting of her hair pulling but had also encouraged her to seek help once again. They became engaged, and the upcoming wedding, with its anticipated attention on her physical appearance, increased her motivation to resolve her hair pulling.

Sharon had recently read an article on trichotillomania in a women's journal that briefly mentioned options for medication treatment. She was skeptical of therapy due to her previous experience, even after other therapeutic techniques specific to trichotillomania were described. Instead, she decided to try medication approaches. She noted that her mother, who had been depressed and had cleaning obsessions, had benefited from treatment with fluoxetine. Sharon herself was prone to minor compulsive behaviors of arranging things symmetrically and described herself as worried, tense, and anxious most of the time.

Fluoxetine was prescribed after the potential benefits and side effects were reviewed. After three weeks Sharon returned to the clinic but reported no improvement in hair pulling. Instead, her hairpulling had actually worsened! Although fluoxetine often diminishes anxiety after a few weeks, in this case Sharon reported increased anxiey and a sense of restlessness. Recognizing this as an occasional side effect of fluoxetine, and a possible factor in her increased hair pulling, her psychiatrist decreased the dose and encouraged her to continue the medication for a few more weeks. Sharon returned a few weeks later, again expressing frustration that the restlessness and hair pulling had not resolved. She indicated that she was ready to leave treatment as it seemed that "nothing would help."

Sharon was reminded that one drug failure didn't mean that another wouldn't work and was encouraged to try another medication. Fluoxetine was stopped and this time sertraline, another SSRI, was prescribed. Over the next few months Sharon noted gradual improvement in her hair pulling with an occasional setback. The sertraline dose was increased on several occasions to see if higher doses would bring better results.

Sharon was initially pleased with her improvement on sertraline but slowly became discouraged by some continued hair pulling as well as a persistent area of scalp hair thinning. Although she didn't want to give up on medication, Sharon wanted to try something new. Her psychiatrist then suggested a trial of clomipramine. Sharon had originally preferred medications other than clomipramine due to her mother's previous experience of side effects with an antidepressant similar to clomipramine.

Sharon's sertraline was tapered off and clomipramine was started. The clomipramine was gradually increased over the next two months. Although Sharon experienced some nuisance side effects, such as mild constipation and sedation, these eventually subsided. She also experienced a persistent mild dry mouth but she found that occasionally sucking on sugarless candies helped to relieve this. Most importantly, Sharon found that her hair pulling diminished almost to zero and that her formerly thin hair was nearly completely filled in after four months. In addition, she found herself less prone to anxiety and compulsions of symmetry.

Side Effects, Doses, and Durations

What are the side effects of clomipramine and the SSRIs? First of all, it should be emphasized that both clomipramine and the SSRIs are very safe drugs. Like all medications, they certainly do have side effects. However, typically these are more in the way of "nuisance effects" than serious problems, particularly in the case of the SSRIs. Furthermore, it is crucial to note that these agents are not addictive, so they can be stopped at any time if a side effect occurs.

Clomipramine and the SSRIs tend to have a slightly different picture of associated "nuisance effects." With clomipramine, dry mouth, constipation, light-headedness, and blurred vision are not uncommon, particularly when higher doses of medication are used. Increased sedation is sometimes seen with clomipramine, although this may disappear with continued use. Clomipramine, more than the SSRIs, can be dangerous when used in quantities greater than that prescribed by a physician.

With the SSRIs, people may notice nausea, change in sleeping pattern, headache, or an increase in anxiety, although these side effects often disappear after a week or two. Both clomipramine and the SSRIs may be associated with changes in weight, decreases in libido, sweating, or difficulty reaching orgasm. Other "nuisance effects" can also be seen, but are less common.

Given that the SSRIs tend to have fewer side effects than clomipramine, it is not uncommon for psychiatrists to begin the treatment of both OCD and hair pulling with one of these agents. On the other hand, if a person does not respond to one or more of the SSRIs, or when a person is willing to try only one medication, then using clomipramine may be an effective strategy. It is important, however, to use any one medication at sufficiently high doses, and for a sufficiently lengthy period of time, before switching to another medication.

In OCD, for example, there is some evidence to suggest that the response to a serotonin reuptake inhibitor may only occur at higher doses of medication than those typically used in the treatment of depression. Thus, there is some rationale for also trying higher than usual doses of medication when treating trichotillomania. Unfortunately, with higher doses of medication, side effects are more likely to be seen. Clomipramine is rarely used at very high doses (greater than 250mg), as more serious side effects can be seen in this dosage range. The SSRIs, however, remain safe even at very high doses.

In addition to the medication dose, another important concern is the length of time necessary before a given medication starts working. In OCD, response to either clomipramine or the SSRIs may be seen only after about ten weeks. In hair pulling, treatment response can often be seen much earlier. However, because of their experience with OCD, psychiatrists usually suggest a relatively long trial of medication, often ten to twelve weeks, to determine carefully whether a specific agent is helpful for hair pulling or not.

When hair pulling does respond to a serotonin reuptake blocker, the next question is how long should the medication be continued. Unfortunately, there are very few studies to help answer this question. In both depression and OCD, however, these agents are often continued for at least a year. Furthermore, in OCD there is some evidence that patients who receive cognitive behavioral therapy are more likely to be able to taper medication without relapse. If there is a medication response, we prefer to see the patient actively involved in cognitive behavioral treatment before tapering their medication after a year or so of drug treatment.

Lithium and Naltrexone

We have already noted that neurotransmitters other than serotonin may be involved in hair pulling. Indeed, although there has been an emphasis on the study of serotonin reuptake inhibitors for the treatment of trichotillomania, several other medications acting on different brain chemical systems have also been shown to be useful in some people with hair pulling. These agents include lithium and naltrexone. When a person fails to respond to the serotonin reuptake inhibitors, these medications should therefore be considered.

Lithium is commonly used in the treatment of people with bipolar disorder (also known as manic-depressive disorder), depression, and other mood and impulse control disorders. It was also found to be useful in an early study of medication treatment for trichotillomania. Lithium should be given strong consideration when the person with trichotillomania fails to respond to a serotonin reuptake inhibitor, or has symptoms that are known to respond to lithium (such as mood and impulse control problems).

Lithium does, however, require close medical monitoring. Possible side effects include changes in the body's blood cells, serum chemistry, kidney function, and thyroid function. It is useful not only to monitor such changes, but also to measure levels of lithium in the blood in order to optimize the dosage used. As a result, lithium is more commonly prescribed by psychiatrists than by family practitioners or other physicians.

Naltrexone is a medication that works on the opioid system in the brain. In the previous chapter we noted that opioids are pleasure-inducing drugs. We also mentioned that certain kinds of opioids may be released in the brain when the body is in pain, and that these agents may also be released during repetitive self-injurious behaviors. Naltrexone has been found to be useful in treating a range of self-injurious behaviors, including hair pulling, as evidenced by the results of one small study. It has also been found useful in certain other conditions, such as alcohol dependence and post-traumatic stress disorder.

Naltrexone tends to have few side effects. Nevertheless, it is currently not widely prescribed by physicians other than psychiatrists. You should not take naltrexone if you have been taking either prescription or nonprescription drugs that contain opiates. It is common for physicians to check your blood for liver abnormalities when initially starting this medication. Naltrexone may be used for hair pulling when the serotonin reuptake inhibitors fail or when the person with hair pulling also has symptoms for which naltrexone can be effective, such as alcohol dependence.

Augmentation Strategies

It is not uncommon for a person with hair pulling to respond only partially, rather than completely, to a particular serotonin reuptake inhibitor. In such cases, it is an option to switch to a different serotonin reuptake blocker, or to a completely different kind of agent such as lithium or naltrexone. An alternative option, however, is to add a second medication to the first medication to enhance its effectiveness. This strategy is called *augmentation*.

Several different medications are potentially useful as augmenting agents for the serotonin reuptake inhibitors in the treatment of hair pulling. Included among these agents are those that act to block the dopamine system (e.g., pimozide or risperidone) and those that may be useful independently in reducing hair pulling (e.g., lithium or naltrexone).

In OCD, it has been shown that those patients who also have tics often require augmentation of the serotonin reuptake inhibitors with low doses of dopamine blockers (e.g., haloperidol and pimozide). There is also some evidence that this augmentation strategy is useful for hair pulling. Unfortunately, many dopamine blockers, particularly when used for a lengthy period of time, may lead to distressing side effects, such as involuntary muscle movements. This augmentation strategy is therefore typically reserved for severe cases of hair pulling.

More recently, however, a number of dopamine blockers (sometimes called *atypical neuroleptics*) have been introduced that may have a safer side effect profile than the older agents (known as *typical neuroleptics*). Recent reports suggest that serotonin reuptake inhibitors, together with low doses of atypical neuroleptics (such as olanzapine or risperidone), may be effective in hair pulling. More rigorous research is necessary to confirm these findings and to document the safety of this combination of agents. In the interim, this augmentation strategy can be considered for severe hair pulling, or for those individuals with both hair pulling and tics.

Lithium and naltrexone may also be prescribed together with a serotonin reuptake inhibitor to further enhance treatment response. Once again, these combinations of medications have not been well studied in hair pulling. Lithium augmentation, however, is known to be useful in the treatment of depression, and should therefore be considered when both hair pulling and depression are present and have responded only partially to serotonin reuptake inhibitors.

When a medication is added to a serotonin reuptake inhibitor as an augmenting agent, it is usually prescribed for only four to six weeks before a decision is made about its effectiveness. Long-term use of augmenting agents has not been well studied. Similar to when serotonin reuptake inhibitors are used alone, an effective augmenting strategy is usually continued for many months and cognitive behavioral treatment is introduced before the medication taper is started. None of the augmenting agents described here are addictive, so that lowering the dose is simple to do.

Managing Side Effects

Fear of side effects is a common reason for choosing not to begin medication or to discontinue medication prematurely. It is important, though, to realize that the side effects of many of the medications most commonly used to treat trichotillomania, especially those of the selective serotonin reuptake inhibitors, are more "nuisance effects" than serious adverse reactions. Furthermore, many of these nuisance effects can be easily managed.

For example, during the first few days of taking a serotonin reuptake blocker, many people experience side effects such as nausea, change in sleep pattern (sleeping too much or too little), or increased anxiety. These side effects often disappear over the next week or two. Taking the medication with meals may be helpful in combating nausea, while changing the timing of the dose (e.g., switching from night to early morning) may be useful in normalizing sleep pattern. For increased anxiety, it may be necessary to decrease the initial dose for a while, or to add an antianxiety medication.

Other common side effects include changes in weight, decreased libido, or difficulty reaching orgasm. These may also decrease over time or may by reduced by lowering the dose of a medication. Several other strategies may also be useful in normalizing sexual function, including changing the timing of the dose (for example, stopping the drug prior to the weekend when sexual activity is more likely) or by adding additional specific medications.

Under the heading of side effects you should also consider the issue of drug interactions. Most medications can, in fact, be safely used along with the selective serotonin reuptake inhibitors. Similarly, although one glass of alcohol may feel like more than just one glass when using these agents, social drinking (e.g. one to two drinks, once or twice a week) is usually possible. Nevertheless, some medications do interact with agents such as the selective serotonin reuptake inhibitors. Therefore, it is wise to check with your physician or pharmacist before taking any new combination of medications. Make sure your physician knows if you are using any herbal preparations. Suddenly stopping medications can also result in side effects and should only be done under the direction of your doctor. Finally, medication should be avoided, if possible, during pregnancy and breast feeding (although certain agents can be relatively safe even during these times).

In general, medication side effects can most often be managed by simple steps, such as waiting for them to disappear spontaneously, reducing the dose of the medication, or making a simple lifestyle change (e.g., taking the medication with meals or at a different time of day). More rarely, it may be necessary to add a second medication to reverse the negative effects of the original medication.

A bottom-line principle in medicine is that side effects should not be worse than the condition for which they were prescribed. While most side effects can be easily managed, there are a number of adverse reactions (e.g., allergic skin rashes) where the best management is to discontinue the offending medication. Thus, when side effects persist despite attempts to reduce them, and when they continue to cause distress or disruption to your lifestyle, it makes sense to look for an alternative medication or different treatment.

Should I Be Taking Medication?

What are the major pros and cons of medication? On the one hand, medication may be a quick and safe way of decreasing hair pulling. On the other hand, any one medication has only a chance of working effectively, so that several months of trying a number of different agents may be needed in order to achieve success.

What about side effects? It might be argued that these are a reason to avoid medication treatments. Certainly, the reality of side effects cannot be denied, but we believe that most of these can be managed without much trouble. Thus, we do not regard side effects of medications such as the SSRIs as a major drawback.

Isn't medication a crutch? Certainly, many people are reluctant to have to rely on an outside agent to control their own symptoms. We would argue, however, that a responsible choice to use medication, or to combine medication with psychotherapy, in fact means taking responsibility for dealing with your problems. From our perspective, medication is most definitely not a sign of weakness or failure!

In general, we are willing to prescribe appropriate medication to anyone who feels sufficiently distressed by their hair pulling to seek this form of treatment. The more severe the hair pulling, the worse the distress, and the greater the interference with the person's life, the more likely we are to support the decision to try medication. Finally, when a person suffers not only from hair pulling but also from another condition, such as a mood or anxiety disorder that also responds to medications prescribed for hair pulling, we are then particularly willing to encourage the use of such agents.

Summary Points

➤ The serotonin reuptake inhibitors are the most commonly used agents for treating hair pulling. Either clomipramine (which may be more effective but may have more side effects) or one of the SSRIs may be tried first.

➤ When the serotonin reuptake inhibitors fail, other medications such as lithium or naltrexone may be tried. When the serotonin reuptake inhbitors are only partially effective, adding a second medication (an augmentation strategy) may be useful.

➤ The selective serotonin reuptake inhibitors are very safe agents. While they do cause "nuisance effects" in some people, these can usually be easily managed. However, you should check before combining these agents with other medications. Medication should only be taken during pregnancy or breast feeding after careful consideration and consultation with a physician.

➤ The serotonin reuptake inhibitors are not addicting and they are not a crutch. The most disadvantageous aspect of taking them for hair pulling is that any one agent has only a limited chance of being effective. Several months of trying a number of different agents may be needed before success is achieved.

Chapter 5

Psychological Treatments for Hair Pulling

In the next few chapters, we will discuss the different kinds of psychological interventions used to treat hair pulling. This chapter will primarily provide an overview of behavioral and cognitive techniques. We will discuss these approaches separately, although they are often used in conjunction with each other and called *cognitive behavioral therapy* (CBT). Each of these approaches has its own particular model to explain how symptoms originate and how best to control problem behaviors. In chapters 6 and 7, you will learn how to use behavioral and cognitive techniques for better control over your hair pulling.

We will also briefly summarize both hypnosis and psychodynamic psychotherapy for hair pulling. Both of these treatments require the involvement of a mental health professional. Behavioral and cognitive techniques, however, can at times be used by the individual hair puller alone. While case studies and anecdotal evidence exist to support the effectiveness of hypnosis for hair pulling, no controlled studies to date have examined this approach. It is our clinical experience that it can be effective in some cases, although we recommend the use of behavioral and cognitive approaches first.

We will mention psychodynamic psychotherapy so that you are aware of this approach. Although there is no research evidence to indicate that psychodynamic approaches are useful in treating trichotillomania, we discuss them here so that you can differentiate treatments. Also, there can be some overlap between certain kinds of cognitive behavioral treatment and some psychodynamic approaches. Psychodynamic psychotherapy may be a useful adjunct for those hair pullers who experience a range of relationship problems (but not as a specific treatment for hair pulling alone).

What Is Behavior Therapy?

Behavior therapy is a treatment approach linked to the school of psychology known as *behaviorism*. It has been very influential in academic psychology for much of this century. Behaviorism has had a number of famous proponents, including psychologists Ivan Pavlov and B. F. Skinner. Behaviorists are primarily interested in environmental factors that either trigger specific behaviors or provide reinforcement or punishment for these behaviors.

For example, behaviorists have noted that when an action is *reinforced* (i.e., followed by a positive consequence or reward such as food, pleasurable experiences, or money), the action tends to be repeated. Conversely, when an action is "punished" (i.e., followed by a negative consequence such as criticism or loss of privileges), the action tends to occur less often and may eventually stop altogether. We should note here that behaviorists use the term *punishment* more broadly than it might be used in everyday conversation. Punishment simply refers to any consequence of a behavior that makes the behavior less likely to occur in the future. Certain forms of behavioral punishment can be very effective in changing behavior without necessarily being disagreeable. The effects of reinforcement and punishment on behavior make up the principles of the behavioral process referred to as *operant conditioning*.

Behaviorists have also noted that environmental cues, which initially have little or no effect on a behavior, can later come to influence that same behavior through the process of *conditioning*. You may be familiar with the example of the Russian scientist Ivan Pavlov, who conducted an experiment in which he served food to a dog only after a bell was rung. Initially the dog would salivate only upon the presentation of food. By pairing the bell with the food, Pavlov was able to make the dog salivate simply by ringing the bell. This method of bringing about behavioral change is referred to as *classical conditioning*. Classical conditioning is not limited to the laboratory but is experienced by human beings all the time. To illustrate this point, ask yourself the question: Have you ever found your mouth watering by just thinking of chocolate chip cookies, pizza, or another favorite food item? Now that you understand some of the theoretical models underlying behavior therapy, let's discuss the application of these principles through behavioral techniques.

How Are Behavioral Principles Used in Practice?

Behavior therapy typically involves the application of techniques designed to change the way people respond to specific stimuli (after the triggering stimuli have been identified). To illustrate, let's discuss an example involving obsessive-compulsive disorder (OCD). People with OCD who experience contamination concerns may wash their hands excessively. Exposure to dirt triggers a high level of anxiety, which, in turn, often leads to hand washing in order to temporarily reduce this discomfort. Hand washing is therefore rewarding, not in the sense that the person necessarily receives pleasure from it, but because uncomfortable feelings are temporarily reduced or eliminated.

Behaviorists call this particular kind of reward *negative reinforcement*. The repeated recurrence of the negative reinforcement increases the likelihood that the person will continue to wash his or her hands under similar circumstances in the future. Repeated hand washing prevents the person from learning that touching things, even dirty things, usually doesn't lead to sickness or other imagined negative consequences. In such a case, the behaviorist would attempt to treat the individual by guiding them through a process in which this behavioral sequence is unlearned.

The specific treatment developed for obsessive-compulsive disorder is called *exposure and response prevention*. With the patient's permission, the therapist gradually exposes him or her to dirt and other feared stimuli, while preventing the patient from engaging in hand washing. At first the patient will become anxious, likely even more anxious than he or she felt before starting therapy. But then an interesting phenomenon occurs: since the hand washing is no longer being reinforced, it begins to decrease in frequency. At the same time, although at a slower rate, the person relearns that some degree of dirt and untidiness is tolerable and does not result in the feared negative consequences.

The behavioral process known as *habituation* is involved here. As people are continuously exposed to something that generates anxiety or discomfort, but doesn't actually result in anticipated problems, they gradually pay less attention to it. An example of this principle is the noise level in the office building of one of the authors. In this particular building, medical charts are transported by carts that travel along a motorized track routed directly over the ceiling. The sound that is produced mimics that of someone vacuuming the floor above. Initially, the sound was quite annoying to the staff. However, after months of exposure, the staff became less aware of, and less irritated by, the noise. In contrast, however, newcomers to the office often comment on how difficult it must be to put up with this noise. In a similar way, as the OCD patient is repeatedly exposed to dirt and germs, the associated anxiety diminishes over time. The expected outcome of treatment would be that patients no longer wash their hands repeatedly, though they may still experience infrequent and mild thoughts of germs (which can now be more readily ignored).

So how does all of this apply to your problem with hair pulling? In the case of hair pulling, behavioral techniques utilizing some of the same principles have been developed. The behavioral techniques employed by different therapists may vary somewhat. Some therapists use individual techniques exclusively. Others combine several different techniques, sometimes with other types of therapy such as hypnosis. Some techniques are more suitable for specific cases of hair pulling, such as in very young children or in cases involving developmental abnormalities.

The most popular behavioral treatment used today is called *habit reversal*. This treatment approach was developed by behavior therapists Nathan Azrin and R. Gregory Nunn (1977) to treat a variety of habitual behaviors, including hair pulling. Habit reversal may also be useful for the treatment of involuntary muscle twitches referred to as tics. Motor and vocal tics are the main behaviors of the disease know as Tourette's disorder. This is of interest as some researchers have conceptualized hair pulling as being similar to tics, though not quite identical. Habit reversal is a multicomponent treatment approach originally designed to include thirteen individual techniques. This treatment approach requires motivation, self-discipline, and perseverance for it to be successful. It is appropriate for use with adolescents and adults, as well as with some older children. Several of the core techniques deserve brief mention here.

One of the first steps to habit reversal is the identification of those environmental stimuli and situations associated with urges to pull and with hair pulling itself. This step is similar to identifying those stimuli that trigger an OCD patient to engage in their compulsions (e.g., for our sample patient it would be dirt and germs that cause the hand washing). This is generally accomplished by maintaining a hair-pulling diary or log, as well as completing several exercises designed to enhance understanding of when and how one's hair pulling occurs. Exercises in chapters 2 and 6 are designed to help you identify these variables for yourself.

After the common triggers for hair pulling have been identified, a new harmless motor behavior, the *competing response*, is substituted for the hair pulling. Competing responses, which are generally quite simple, must be incompatible with hair extraction. Examples include clenching one's fist and stroking or squeezing a Koosh Ball (a rubber ball with many slender, hair-like projections). In both cases, the hand is occupied and is unable to grasp hair. This competing or incompatible response can be used either to interrupt a hair-pulling episode or to prevent hair pulling from occurring.

Additionally, since hair pulling often occurs in situations characterized by tension or anxiety, instruction in diaphragmatic breathing and/or relaxation techniques is also central to habit reversal (see chapter 7). There exists a myriad of ways in which to learn relaxation techniques. You should sample several different approaches and choose the method most suitable for you. Other habit reversal techniques include graphing progress and using the support of a family member or friend. All of these approaches will make more sense in the next two chapters, where we will describe in detail habit reversal techniques that you can start using at home.

There is increasing evidence that behavior therapy is effective in changing problem behaviors such as hair pulling. Behavioral techniques make common sense, they work quickly, and their effects can be long-lasting. Furthermore, these techniques can be utilized by the hair puller alone, or with the help of a friend or family member acting as a coach. Behavior therapy can be short-term and not involve the costs often associated with medication treatment and follow-up.

Behavior therapy techniques are safe and useful, and should be used by the majority of people with hair pulling.

What Is Cognitive Therapy?

Cognitive psychology addresses the mental events, thoughts, and feelings that occur in response to a stimulus or event in the environment, and precede the person's behavioral response to that stimulus or event. Cognitive theorists argue that by focusing solely on observable events (stimuli and responses), behaviorism fails to account for the contribution of the mind to our behavior. Thus, even though behavior therapy may be successful when the therapist and patient are engaged in treatment, it is successful because cognitive changes are occurring simultaneously with the behavioral changes.

Cognitive psychology is currently a highly popular approach within the field of psychology. The principles of cognitive psychology have been widely tested and applied in the treatment of many different psychiatric disorders. For example, cognitive psychology has noted that people with symptoms of depression often have negative thoughts preceding their depressed mood. These thoughts are often a distortion of the reality and may magnify negative circumstances and minimize or ignore positive events. In addition, they are usually automatic, routine, and habitual, so that the person does not recognize their occurrence. The theory is that the negative thoughts lead directly to the experience of negative feelings.

In the cognitive therapy of depression and anxiety, procedures are used to help sufferers become aware of their negative distortions about themselves, the world, and the future. They are instructed to restructure their thoughts in more positive, accurate, and functional ways. Several rigorously conducted scientific studies have demonstrated the effectiveness of cognitive techniques in alleviating depressed mood and anxiety.

Cognitive therapy techniques for hair pulling are primarily used to target specific negative or maladaptive thoughts related to the hair pulling itself. However, since depression and anxiety are often components of the hair pulling experience, cognitive techniques can also be used to lessen depression and anxiety. Let's proceed now to a discussion of some specific cognitive techniques for use in the treatment of chronic hair pulling.

How Does Cognitive Therapy Work in Practice?

Cognitive therapy generally involves the identification of one's automatic negative thoughts and efforts to change them. Psychologist Vicky Gluhoski (1995) has suggested that the cognitive distortions involved in hair pulling can fall into one of three categories. One category addresses the hair puller's beliefs about the value of hair pulling. For example, if individuals tell themselves "I can't cope without hair pulling," the problem behavior is likely to persist.

Another category of cognitive distortion involves automatic thoughts about specific situations that produce negative feelings. In this case, if hair pullers tell themselves that a situation will overwhelm them, they are likely to engage in pulling for relief or comfort.

Lastly, thoughts that provide permission for the problem behavior (e.g., "I'll only pull one hair and then stop") allow the puller to initiate the behavior. Various techniques are used to identify the problematic thoughts, including keeping a diary of your thoughts. The next step is to challenge these negative thoughts with actual data and alternative explanations.

Let's look at a clinical example to illustrate the steps in cognitive therapy. During the course of a therapy session for depression, Mary reported a recent event in which she felt rejected, hurt, and ultimately depressed. She described how a valued friend had failed to greet her when passing her in the hall. After some reflection, Mary was able to identify the automatic thought that her friend intentionally chose to avoid eye contact, either because she was mad at Mary or growing tired of her company. This led Mary to experience additional negative thoughts about presumed defects in her character that made her undesirable both as a friend and as a person in general. However, when Mary was asked to describe the incident in more detail during treatment, she recalled noting that her friend appeared rushed and preoccupied at the time. In fact, Mary even recalled her friend brushing against someone further down the hall as if she was not paying much attention to her environment. Mary was then able to suggest a more plausible explanation for the event: that her friend hadn't noticed her because she was preoccupied and, most likely, had no intention of avoiding her. As a result, Mary no longer felt as rejected or as depressed over this occurrence, since her thoughts were no longer as consistent with these negative emotions.

Cognitive therapists use real-life events such as the one just described to teach people how to become more aware of what is going on around them, how they are prone to think about these events, and how these events affect the way they feel. There are a number of self-help books based on cognitive therapy principles for depression and anxiety that are available in most bookstores and certainly through the Internet. These provide a good groundwork for learning and applying these techniques to your daily experiences. However, extensive change of automatic thoughts is likely to require dedicated practice and possibly initial direction from a trained therapist.

Let's discuss now how cognitive therapy techniques have been applied to the treatment of hair pulling. Cognitive therapists ask their patients to note all thoughts and feelings that occur immediately prior to, during, and after hair pulling. For example, it may be the case that thoughts about failure or feelings of anxiety are found to consistently precede hair pulling. These thoughts and feelings are then explored in greater depth in order to determine their origins and challenge any distorted automatic thinking. Finally, the client and therapist work to change the thoughts and feelings that promote the hair pulling.

A simple but extremely useful cognitive therapy tool is the daily thought record. These records can be used to specify the automatic thoughts, feelings, and intensity of emotion when the hair pulling urges and behavior occur. Restructured thoughts are then also written down and the intensity of the emotion is reevaluated after the cognitive restructuring occurs. The individuals then learn how to reformulate their thoughts and, thus, reduce the negative emotions that historically triggered the hair pulling.

One of our hair pullers, Susan, notes that she generally has an increase in anxiety (experienced as a feeling of butterflies in her stomach) prior to pulling her hair. Susan rated the level of her anxiety as approximately 60 (on a scale of 0 to 100). By focusing on her thoughts, she caught herself thinking that she was unable to control things at work. In this case Susan reminded herself that her coworkers think of her as a competent worker, and that, in fact, she typically manages things just fine. Additionally, a recent performance review had consistently good marks. After dwelling on this a bit longer, she reassessed her level of anxiety and noted that it fell to a level of about 30. As the level of anxiety decreased, the urges to hair pull also diminished. This case highlights how tension, anxiety, and depression can play an important role in hair pulling. It also illustrates how cognitive approaches can reduce these emotions directly and, subsequently, decrease hair pulling.

Cognitive techniques can also target thoughts more specific to hair pulling:

For example, one of our patients, Fran, a twenty-three- year-old dental hygienist with a twelve-year history of hair pulling, was maintaining a hair-pulling diary of events, thoughts, and emotions, as well as her hair-pulling behavior. She came to one session expressing frustration over her progress. She stated that her hair pulling was just as frequent and severe as when treatment began. She felt that she had no control over her behavior and worried that she would always be this way. Furthermore, she stated that she might as well quit treatment altogether and just accept that she was a shameful hair puller. Obviously, these thoughts had a negative impact on her mood. In exploring these thoughts, she was asked how she had concluded that she wasn't getting better. She was encouraged to look at sources of information that might present an accurate reflection of her progress.

Together with the therapist, Fran graphed the number of hair pulling episodes and hairs pulled each week for the several months she had been in treatment. Fran was indeed surprised to discover that the graph had a downward trend and that she was pulling 50 percent less than when treatment first started. Additionally, she was pulling out about half as much hair when she did have a hair-pulling episode. This example is similar to how one can view a glass as either half empty or half full. In the case of Fran, her initial impression was of a completely empty glass. Such extreme distorted thinking is referred to in cognitive therapy as *catastrophizing*. After recognition of her progress, Fran found that her associated feelings had subsequently changed. The frustration and depression present at the beginning of the session were since replaced by more optimism and pride.

Cognitive interventions have been shown to be effective in a number of conditions. Once again, they fit well with commonsense principles, work quickly, and can have a long-lasting effect. However, cognitive therapy techniques per se have not been well-studied in trichotillomania. Generally they have been included in treatment packages along with behavioral techniques and the therapy, as a whole, has been shown to be effective. Nevertheless, it may be useful to add simple cognitive therapy techniques to any attempt to control hair pulling. Cognitive therapy may be particularly useful when a person with hair pulling also has another condition, such as depression or an anxiety disorder (see chapter 2), which respond well to cognitive therapy.

What About Hypnosis?

Hypnotherapists employ altered states of consciousness in order to explore the unconscious or to change behavior. Altered states of consciousness are, in fact, an ordinary part of life. We alter our state of consciousness when we relax deeply, when we concentrate intensely, or when we fall asleep. Hypnotherapists are trained psychotherapists who employ such techniques to treat a specific problem. It is important to note that they should be clearly differentiated from hypnotists or other lay persons who use hypnotic techniques with clients but who have no formal training.

Once the person is in an altered state of consciousness, otherwise know as a *trance,* he or she may be able to access thoughts and feelings more readily and be more susceptible to therapeutic suggestions. Thus, during a trance, the person may be able to connect current symptoms with past events, and may begin to follow instructions from the hypnotherapist to decrease the problematic behaviors. Hypnotherapy has been shown to be useful in a number of conditions, including various kinds of habits. Although there are few rigorous studies of hypnotherapy in trichotillomania, several individual case reports and case series describe it as very useful in reducing hair pulling for some individuals.

In general, the first step in hypnosis is being guided into a hypnotic trance. In the case of hair pulling, once trance induction has been mastered, some hypnotherapists then explore associations or memories related to the hair pulling. Most hypnotherapists utilize the hypnotic trance as a channel for encouraging the person to replace the hair pulling with other more adaptive behaviors. Some of the suggestions that have been used include:

- increased awareness of hair pulling

- greater control of hair pulling

- increased pain from hair pulling

- reduced anxiety and, thus, less need to pull out hair

- greater respect for one's body

- substitution of hair pulling with a more adaptive behavior

The hair puller would then be encouraged to practice trance induction and autosuggestion at home. Frequently this is done with the aid of a tape made during one of the sessions. Hypnotherapists usually recommend listening to this tape once or more a day. Typically hypnosis treatment of hair pulling involves a limited number of sessions, with follow-up booster sessions upon completion of the treatment.

What About Psychodynamic Psychotherapy?

Psychodynamic psychotherapy is a form of therapy that focuses on the unconscious and the past causes of one's current mental life. Many of its seminal theories were originally formulated by Sigmund Freud. These theories have undergone subsequent modification so that today there exist many different schools of thought within psychodynamic psychotherapy.

Psychodynamic psychotherapists maintain that current symptoms often have unconscious origins. It is also believed that the relationship between the client and the therapist may reflect aspects of the client's important relationships early on in life. As the therapy progresses, the goal is for the client to learn about the underlying meanings of current symptoms and behaviors, partly by relating these to past experiences. Theoretically this developing insight is expected to facilitate behavioral change.

Typically clients in psychodynamic psychotherapy follow the classic psychoanalytic rule of talking about what is foremost in their minds. At the beginning of the therapy, the psychotherapist may take a detailed history of the past including early childhood and the family background. Later on the therapist may draw connections between current behaviors and relationships and the patient's past history.

In the case of trichotillomania, psychodynamic psychotherapists may try to establish the unconscious meanings of pulling out hair. For example, hair often symbolizes beauty, so pulling out hair may be interpreted to reflect an unconscious wish to be less beautiful. Hair can also symbolize maturity and/or femininity; thus, hair pulling may also be interpreted to reflect a desire to maintain childhood or deny femininity. Hair cutting has often been used in societies to indicate mourning, as a form of punishment, or to signify wrongdoing. Accordingly, hair pulling may be viewed as symbolizing grief or an unconscious desire to punish oneself. Many other symbolic representations of hair have also been proposed. It is important to remember that hair may symbolize drastically different things to different people.

There are no studies that support psychodynamic approaches as being useful in stopping hair pulling as such. Indeed, for many or even most people with hair pulling, it is quite plausible that hair pulling has no symbolic meaning at all. In our (admittedly anecdotal) experience, some hair pullers have noted that psychodynamic approaches have resulted in harmful outcomes when they were interpreted to have sexual conflicts or labeled as masochistic because they extracted their hair. On the other hand, there are similarities between some forms of cognitive behavioral treatment and certain schools of psychodynamic psychotherapy. These kinds of approaches may well be useful for hair pullers who also have other kinds of problems, particularly interpersonal difficulties.

Research to Date

Unfortunately, the research addressing psychological approaches for the treatment of hair pulling has been limited. Much of the early literature on this subject was authored by psychodynamic psychotherapists. Although they reported successful treatment outcomes in individual cases, it is important to note that psychodynamic approaches have not been subject to rigorous research study.

More recently behavior therapists have increasingly documented their success in treating hair pulling. However, few behavior therapists have employed identical techniques, making it difficult to compare interventions and determine which techniques show greater promise. Some of this work is rigorous and convincing, and comprises the only well-controlled research of psychological treatments for hair pulling. Habit reversal, a multicomponent treatment approach, has been studied in the most detail and the research to date demonstrates this approach to be effective.

Finally, existing case reports indicate that hypnotherapy can be useful for some people with hair pulling. In a few cases, people who had earlier failed to respond to behavior therapy and medication had later responded to hypnotherapy. Again, however, there is a lack of rigorous research that clearly demonstrates the effectiveness of hypnotherapy. Hypnotherapy should therefore be considered only when other interventions (such as behavior or cognitive therapies or medication) have failed.

In summary, more careful research on the psychological treatments for hair pulling is clearly needed. We strongly recommend habit reversal for all hair pullers given the existence of empirical demonstration of its efficacy. While little research exists on cognitive approaches alone, cognitive techniques have often been included in treatment packages with reported success. In the absence of data to document efficacy with psychodynamic psychotherapy, we do not recommend this treatment approach as an intervention targeted to treat hair pulling alone. In addition, it can be quite costly and time-consuming, and some patients actually report negative secondary effects to some of the more common interpretations of their hair-pulling symptoms.

Although no one is yet able to say with certainty who will respond to which kind of psychotherapy, it is possible to formulate some general approaches for using psychotherapy techniques. We discuss these in the next section.

How Do You Choose Among the Available Treatments?

There are a number of reasons to use psychological techniques for hair pulling. Many hair pullers much prefer the idea of changing their behavior by greater awareness and learning specific techniques, rather than by taking medications. Furthermore, unless hair pulling is accompanied by other symptoms or problems that are overlooked during treatment, psychological approaches are a very safe form of treatment. Behavior therapy not only appears to be effective, but it is also the easiest form of treatment to learn about and to practice on your own. Thus, it is our recommendation that behavior therapy techniques should be used by the majority of people with hair pulling.

Cognitive therapy is not as easy to carry out without the help of a therapist. However, some cognitive therapy techniques, such as thought records, are easy to learn about and to practice on your own. When hair pulling is accompanied by problems such as depression or an anxiety disorder, it may be particularly helpful to consult a trained cognitive therapist.

Hypnotherapy also requires seeing a skilled therapist (don't consult anyone who is not also a licensed psychotherapist!). However, hypnotherapy may well be worth the effort for people whose hair pulling has not responded to other kinds of treatments. We strongly encourage you to find a hypnotherapist who has had previous experience in treating hair pulling if you decide to pursue this approach.

Psychodynamic psychotherapy is often considered to be attractive by those individuals interested in understanding themselves better and furthering self-development. However, there is relatively little evidence that this form of psychotherapy helps with hair pulling per se. It usually involves a long-term commitment and is therefore relatively expensive. However, intensive psychodynamically-based treatments can be useful for those hair pullers who also present with other psychological issues.

Complete the following checklist to help you identify which treatment approaches (i.e., psychological and/or medication) may be the best individualized treatment for you. It is our recommendation that medication treatments be considered for use in conjunction with psychological approaches when hair loss is severe; the puller is significantly distressed by the problem; the pulling significantly impacts social, leisure, or occupational functioning; and/or there is significant co-occurring depression or anxiety.

Exercise: Identifying Factors Important for Treatment Selection

Below is a list of questions that will be useful for you to consider when deciding on which treatment approach(es) you select. It will help you to decide among psychological approaches as well as whether to consider use of medications. Check off "Yes" or "No" for each item.

	Yes	No
Is there visible hair loss?	____	____
Are you seriously distressed by your pulling?	____	____
Do you avoid social activities due to your pulling?	____	____
Do you avoid leisure activities due to your pulling?	____	____

Do you avoid occupational activities due to your
pulling?   _____   _____

Does your pulling cause tension in your
relationships?   _____   _____

Do you pull in front of your children or others?   _____   _____

Are you depressed or irritable much of the time?   _____   _____

Are you anxious much of the time?   _____   _____

Do you have any other psychological problems that
affect your hair pulling?   _____   _____

Have you been treated for psychological problems
other than hair pulling in the past?   _____   _____

Do you have a history of childhood trauma or
deprivation?   _____   _____

Do you have any interpersonal difficulties that cause
you distress or impair your functioning?   _____   _____

Do you have a history of medication sensitivity?   _____   _____

Have you previously tried some of the medications
used for hair pulling without success?   _____   _____

Are you willing to take medications as
recommended?   _____   _____

Are you able to afford the costs involved in
medication or psychological treatments?   _____   _____

Do you have religious, cultural, or personal beliefs
that prevent medication use?   _____   _____

Are you currently pregnant or do you plan on
becoming pregnant in the near future?   _____   _____

Are you on other medications or do you have any
physical problems that may interact with medication
use?   _____   _____

Do you have reasonable expectations for treatment
outcome with medications?   _____   _____

	Yes	No
Are you willing to make the commitment and spend the time necessary to practice behavioral techniques?	___	___
Are you willing to tolerate the discomfort that results from resisting urges with behavioral treatment?	___	___
Do you have reasonable expectations for outcome with behavioral or cognitive approaches?	___	___
Do you believe in the value of hypnosis?	___	___
Do you have reasonable expectations for outcome with hypnosis?	___	___

Note: No single formula exists to determine which treatment approach would be the best for any individual hair puller. It is our hope that by reflecting on the answers to the questions above, you will gain some insight into what would be a good treatment match for you.

Summary Points

▶ Behavior therapy, cognitive therapy, psychodynamic therapy, and hypnotherapy all have different models for the causes and treatment of hair pulling.

▶ Behavior therapy is safe and often effective for hair pulling.

▶ Behavior therapy techniques are relatively easy to learn and practice on your own. We recommend their use by the majority of individuals with hair pulling.

▶ Some cognitive therapy techniques are also easy to learn and practice without the involvement of a trained professional. A cognitive therapist should be strongly considered when co-occurring depression or anxiety is present. Cognitive approaches can also be used for distorted thinking directly associated with hair pulling.

▶ Hypnotherapy may be useful when other forms of psychological treatment have failed.

➤ Insufficient evidence exists at present to recommend psychodynamic psychotherapy alone for the treatment of hair pulling. However, psychodynamic psychotherapy may be indicated when hair pullers also experience significant relationship problems.

Chapter 6

Starting to Use Behavior Therapy Techniques

While medications, hypnosis, and other forms of psychotherapy can be helpful, we strongly recommend that you make behavior therapy the foundation of your treatment efforts. You will find behavioral treatment techniques to be simple in theory, easy to learn, and readily practiced at home. Not only does the behavioral approach make common sense, there is growing scientific research to document its effectiveness in the treatment of hair pulling.

Before you start behavior therapy, however, it is important that you make sure that you are ready. Behavioral treatment requires more time and effort than medications or other therapies. Just as your hair pulling developed over time, it will take a while to learn how to better manage the urges and change your behavior. It is important that you have reasonable expectations regarding the necessary time commitment.

While medications may decrease the frequency or intensity of hair-pulling urges, pills cannot change habitual behaviors. This will happen only when you repeatedly practice new ways of handling these triggers for hair pulling. If you are currently depressed or under a lot of stress, you may want to deal with these issues before you begin behavior therapy. You will be asked to actively participate in getting better by doing tasks that are intended to increase your awareness, help you learn your triggers for pulling, and change your habits. Remember, practice makes perfect!

Setting the pace at which you learn new behavioral tools should be an individual decision. You need to be realistic about what you can do. It is better to learn one technique at a time and add new tools after you have mastered the earlier ones. Once you have learned a technique, you need to continue practicing it while you successfully integrate additional tools.

You may encounter pitfalls if you try to implement multiple new techniques at once. It can be quite overwhelming trying to remember several new coping responses. Many techniques will not be beneficial until they have been practiced repeatedly. If you fail to set an individual treatment pace that works for you, you run the risk of discarding tools that could be effective for you with time. You could also prematurely conclude that your case is hopeless. Do you remember the story of the tortoise and the hare? We prefer that you choose to be the tortoise and successfully persist along the road to better management of your hair pulling.

Your expectations regarding the course of progress are also critical to your success with the behavioral approach. As we discussed earlier, trichotillomania has a waxing and waning course so your hair pulling is likely to increase and decrease over time as a function of the many variables that affect it. As we mentioned earlier, hair pulling is generally very reactive to situational stress. Since you can't always know when stress is around the corner, you need to have realistic expectations regarding your ability to successfully use your tools to manage your habit.

In the beginning, you will not always be successful with your efforts at control. Over time, though, your success will improve as you better identify all of the factors that make your hair pulling better or worse. Recognition of these relevant variables will happen with time as you monitor your behavior and test out alternative coping strategies. Thus, while working on getting better, remember to look at the long-term picture, as opposed to the short-term view. Try to focus on your progress and use it to keep you on the right path.

Lastly, it will be important that you tailor your own hair-pulling treatment plan to match the details of your individual hair-pulling habit. Since each hair puller can have a very different pattern, the most successful plan would address the specifics of pulling that characterize your problem. You may discover that awareness-enhancing techniques should be the cornerstone of your plan, or you may decide to emphasize different coping strategies for responding to your hair-pulling triggers. In chapter 2, your self-monitoring exercise helped you to identify your specific hair-pulling "signature," including the triggers that you will need to address actively in your behavioral plan.

Let's now move on to some simple exercises. In this chapter you will largely focus on enhancing motivation, increasing awareness, and maintaining your motivation and awareness throughout the course of treatment. As you work through the following chapters, you should expect some improvement. However, you should also realize that setbacks and slips are an expected part of learning. Don't let these temporary interruptions paralyze you. Focus on your progress and take the setbacks in stride. Ask yourself what lessons you can learn from any setbacks. This will change setbacks into learning experiences that can help you prevent hair pulling in the future.

Enhancing Motivation

The success of behavioral treatment depends on your motivation to actively learn about your habit and consistently practice alternative responses. The fact that you purchased this book and have already read the earlier chapters indicates that you desire to achieve better control over your hair pulling. To further enhance your motivation, it is important that you review the impact hair pulling has had on your life and the reasons why you now want to control it.

Very often hair pullers forget the considerable toll that their problem has taken on their lives. Since your current hair-pulling pattern likely developed over several years, you probably made gradual changes in your life to deal with it. You may have forgotten how you used to enjoy swimming or riding your bicycle on a windy day. Identifying the limitations you suffer as a result of your hair pulling will boost your motivation to take control and tackle your problem.

Current research shows that different hair pullers are affected by their problem in different ways. For many, it is the loss of hair and the negative impact on their physical appearance that causes great distress. For others, it may be the time they lose when engaging in hair pulling, or the loss of self-esteem and decreased sense of control that accompanies hair pulling. Some hair pullers are most disturbed by the negative consequences it has on their interpersonal relationships or the limitations on different activities. This first exercise will help you to outline your individual consequences to your hair-pulling problem.

Exercise: Identifying the Negative Consequences to Your Hair Pulling

Following is a list of many of the common negative outcomes to chronic hair pulling. We have grouped the consequences into several categories. Read through each category and place a check mark in the box preceding those items that apply to you.

Physical Consequences:

☐ Thinning hair

☐ Bald spots

☐ Changes in hair color

☐ Changes in hair texture

☐ Inability to wear certain hairstyles

☐ The need for makeup, hats, etc. to hide damage

☐ Scratches and sores

☐ Skin sensitivity in areas of pulling

☐ Infections

☐ Scarring at pulling sites

☐ Muscle cramping from pulling

☐ Finger calluses from pulling

☐ Stomach upset (if ingest hair)

☐ Other(s) _____

_____

_____

Emotional Consequences:

☐ Shame/embarrassment

☐ Loneliness/isolation

☐ Frustration

☐ Loss of sense of control

☐ Decreased self-esteem

☐ Self-hate

☐ Sadness

☐ Fear of being discovered

☐ Anxiety that children will mimic behavior

☐ Guilt

☐ Worry

☐ Other(s) _____

_____

_____

Economic Consequences:

☐ Cost of wig(s)

☐ Cost of makeup

☐ Cost of hats, scarves, etc.

☐ Cost of specialized hair products

☐ Cost of treatment (psychiatric, dermatologic, etc.)

☐ Other(s) _____

_____

_____

Interpersonal Consequences:

☐ Avoidance of intimate relationships

☐ Fear of rejection

☐ Handling unsolicited questions about hair loss

☐ Receiving unsolicited advice about problem

☐ Arguments over hair pulling

☐ Stress on relationships

☐ Issues of deception and lying about problem

☐ Expressions of disgust or disapproval by others

☐ Avoidance of routine medical visits (e.g., family physician, gynecologist)

☐ Avoidance of routine dental visits (if chew hair)

☐ Avoidance of hair salons/barbershops

☐ Scheduling time apart from partner to pull

◻ Misperceptions of hair loss by others (e.g., chemotherapy)

◻ Other(s) _____

_____

_____

Occupational and Leisure Consequences:

◻ Avoidance of certain professions to limit exposure

◻ Avoidance of job tasks (e.g., talks)

◻ Avoidance of athletic activities (e.g., swimming, biking)

◻ Avoidance of restaurants

◻ Avoidance of sitting in the floor section of a theater

◻ Avoidance of bleachers

◻ Limiting activities on a windy or rainy day

◻ Refusing overnight trips due to limited privacy

◻ Avoidance of sedentary activities where pulling occurs (e.g., television, reading)

◻ Other(s) _____

_____

_____

We're sure that you were able to relate to many of the negative consequences listed. You were also probably able to identify additional outcomes that were not listed. Hopefully this exercise highlighted the importance of efforts to achieve increased control over your hair pulling. We suggest that you keep this list handy and refer back to it from time to time to sustain your motivation. Next we'd like you to try an exercise that will further underscore the limitations you experience as a consequence of your hair pulling.

Exercise: Listing Reasons to Control Your Hair Pulling

Take a minute now to review those items you recognized in the prior exercise. Identify the ten negative consequences that bother you the most. Then specify the corresponding positive changes that might occur if you could control the hair pulling. For example, Jason identified "avoidance of swimming" and "worry that my mom will be upset" as two of his major negative consequences to hair pulling. He wrote down that the positive treatment outcome to controlling his hair pulling would include "being able to go with my friends to the local beach" and "not feeling like I've upset my mom."

Negative Consequence	Positive Treatment Outcome
1. _____	1. _____
_____	_____
2. _____	2. _____
_____	_____
3. _____	3. _____
_____	_____
4. _____	4. _____
_____	_____
5. _____	5. _____
_____	_____
6. _____	6. _____
_____	_____
7. _____	7. _____
_____	_____
8. _____	8. _____
_____	_____
9. _____	9. _____
_____	_____
10. _____	10. _____
_____	_____

Increasing Awareness

Now that you've enhanced your motivation to control your problem, the next step is to develop an increased awareness of your hair-pulling behavior. Your initial reaction may be that you already are always aware of your hair pulling. You're not alone in responding this way! We routinely get this reaction from many of our patients. However, before you decide that this step does not apply to you, stop and ask yourself the following questions:

- Have you ever found yourself touching or stroking your hair unconsciously?

- Have you ever discovered hair in your hand, or piles of hair on the floor, without remembering pulling the hair out (or having pulled more hair than you expected)?

- Have you had the experience of someone else telling you to stop playing with your hair when you were unaware or barely aware that you were doing so?

- Have you ever looked in a mirror and felt shocked to discover thinning hair or bald spots that you did not know existed?

If you responded "yes" to any of these questions, these next exercises will be important treatment steps for you.

In chapter 2 you completed several exercises that helped you pinpoint common triggers for your hair pulling. Self-monitoring your hair pulls and associated triggers is a very effective tool for enhancing awareness of your behavior. An additional task that increases awareness is to reduce your complex hair-pulling routine into the specific sequential motor steps that make up your unique hair-pulling habit.

To help you understand the value of this task, let's consider an analogy with swimming. When individuals first learn to swim, they start off by focusing on the coordination of their breathing with specific motor movements. For example, when you first learn to do the crawl, you practice your breathing in conjunction with the appropriate arm movements. When you master this step, you add the necessary leg movements to the sequence. Once these activities are coordinated and practiced repeatedly, swimming becomes "automatic" and can be done with minimal awareness of the constituent steps. If you later wish to change your swimming technique, you would need to refocus on specific , recoordinate the entire sequence, and then practice until it became automatic again.

Now if you think about hair pulling, it also consists of a sequence of motor movements that are largely reflexive. Unlike swimming, hair pulling did not need to be learned, but probably came naturally to you. In fact, many authorities in this field have suggested that hair pulling mimics a natural grooming process in which normal behaviors have become greatly exaggerated.

As we discussed earlier, complex behaviors can be broken down into a chain of smaller behavioral components. For your hair pulling, we are interested in identifying the many behaviors that precede the final action of hair extraction. If you can identify these earlier steps and interrupt the behavioral chain before you pluck your hair then you will have successfully avoided hair loss!

To further illustrate this point, let's examine the hair-pulling sequence mapped out by Robin. By completing the earlier exercises, Robin had successfully identified that she was most prone to hair pulling when she was alone at night in her room doing homework. She reported sitting on her bed, holding the textbook in her right hand, and using her available left hand to play with her hair. She had discovered that she often found herself worried and tense when she was studying her calculus. She also noted that her hair was more appealing to her at the end of the day when it had an oily feeling. Once she identified these pulling parameters, she began to be more aware of her habit when she studied. When asked to describe the actual sequence of activities involved in her pulling, Robin noted the following pattern:

- Initially I'm sitting up in bed, with my right hand holding the book flat and my left hand holding a magic marker for highlighting.

- My back starts to feel a little sore and I gradually slide down until I am lying on my side on the bed. This position makes me feel more relaxed and comfortable.

- I then reposition my right hand to support the book and I eventually put down the highlighter.

- My left hand rises up and I find myself cupping the left side of my face with my open palm. Occasionally my left hand supports the book while my right hand turns the page, but it always returns to my face.

- When I become particularly absorbed in my reading, my left hand begins to slowly stroke the skin on that side of my face. If I discover any scabs or skin irregularities, I repeatedly stroke them, and may occasionally remove a loose scab.

- After a while my left hand moves up to my hairline and feels around for acne that I often develop in that area. If I find anything, my hand may linger and slowly pick at it.

- In the process of doing this, my bangs often fall down in my face and cover the fingers of my left hand.

- My thumb and left index finger may then grasp several of the hairs that are loose and run up and down the hair shaft.

- These two fingers then separate the hairs while rubbing them against the skin of the fingers. If a particularly coarse or kinky hair is discovered, my fingers will let go of all other hairs but this one.

- Next my fingers will tug several times on the hair without initially extracting it. Finally my hand will tug more strongly and the hair will come out.

- My hand will then bring the hair up to my lips and rub it repetitively across them.

- I will then position the bulb of the hair root between my teeth and bite down on it while pulling the hair out from my mouth.

- I will then roll the hair bulb around inside my mouth with my tongue, eventually swallowing it.

- I will glance down at the hair shaft and examine the hair for its texture and to make sure that the bulb was removed.

- I will then roll the hair between my fingers and discard it on the floor.

By describing each behavioral component to her sequence of hair pulling, Robin successfully identified fifteen motor behaviors preceding the actual hair removal. Each of these steps could then become an actual point of intervention to prevent the later step of hair extraction. By knowing her steps, Robin could identify alternative behaviors to engage in at each juncture.

For example, Robin could identify ways to make herself feel comfortable sitting up in bed so that she does not end up in a prone position (e.g., get a back pillow to use while studying). She could also focus on the positioning of her left hand, making sure that it remained occupied by holding the pen or a toy. She could decrease access to her scalp by wearing a baseball cap, headband, or scarf while studying. She could make her hair less appealing by washing it prior to studying to remove its oily feeling. As you can see, there are many different steps that Robin could take to interrupt her habitual hair-pulling sequence.

By identifying these high-risk motor behaviors and generating alternative responses, Robin can protect herself from engaging in hair-pulling behavior. Furthermore, by thinking in detail about her hair-pulling sequence, she is likely to become even more aware every time that her hand moves in the direction of her scalp. Robin also discovered that there are steps involved in the hair-pulling sequence that occur after the hair has been extracted. Once she recognized that the oral behaviors with the hair root were satisfying and pleasurable, she could identify why she enjoyed this and what alternative behaviors may function as effective substitute behaviors.

Exercise: Outlining Your Hair-Pulling Motor Sequence

Now it's your turn to identify the steps that make up the behavioral sequence to your hair-pulling pattern. In order to record the smaller steps to your hair pulling, observe yourself in a mirror "practicing" your hair-pulling routine. It may also be helpful to pretend that you are instructing a friend in how to replicate your own pattern of hair pulling.

Using the worksheet that follows, write down as many individual behavioral movements as you can to your hair pulling. There are spaces between each step for you to later fill in any additional steps you discover with further exploration. Practice this exercise several times and in different situations. You will find that differences in behavioral sequences may occur from situation to situation. However, undoubtedly there will be similarities across situations. It will be particularly important for you to develop alternatives for these common behavioral steps that universally occur. As you gain increased knowledge of your hair pulling, hopefully you will be more aware of the positioning of your hand both during exercises and when you're not specifically focusing on these tasks. Your greater knowledge should enhance your recognition of, and preparedness for, high-risk situations for hair pulling.

Behavioral Steps in My Hair-Pulling Sequence

1. _____

_____

2. _____

_____

3. _____

_____

4. _____

_____

5. _____

_____

6. _____

_____

7. _____

_____

8. _____

_____

9. _____

_____

10. _____

_____

Now that you have succeeded in outlining your own hair-pulling motor sequence, continue on to complete some additional exercises to strengthen your awareness. It's time to remind you, however, that you should be mindful of the pace with which you undertake these tasks. It's important that you spend sufficient time on each exercise to learn the unique characteristics of your habit. Once again, remember that it took considerable time for your habit to develop. As a result, it will also take time for you to acquire better management of your urges and increased control over your hair pulling.

Exercise: Creating a Visual Record of Your Hair-Pulling Habit

Another method for enhancing your awareness is to take a photographic record over time of the body site(s) where there has been hair-pulling damage. Comparison of recent photographs with pictures taken prior to the onset of the problem will help clarify the extent of physical damage. In addition, pictures can be very useful for purposes of documenting changes over time with treatment. As the saying goes, a picture is worth a thousand words!

It's not unusual for some hair pullers to deny the severity of their habit. Since in some cases the damage can occur slowly over time, it's not surprising that individuals may lose track of how thick their hair was originally. This is not dissimilar to how we fail to notice that we are growing tall as youngsters—it is only when we see a relative or friend whom we haven't seen for years that we become aware of how much we have grown.

Conversely, other hair pullers can have an exaggerated view of the extent of damage incurred from their hair pulling. As a result, they may suffer from lowered self-esteem and avoid many activities. In these cases, viewing actual pictures may help to normalize their perception of the physical damage incurred from their hair pulling.

It will be easiest to take pictures if you have someone you trust assist you in this endeavor. Using a Polaroid or digital camera will be the easiest way to accomplish this task. If you don't have either of these, however, use of a conventional camera is still possible, though it requires your willingness to have your film processed by an outside agency.

We suggest taking photos every four weeks and placing them in a notebook with the date. Given the rate at which hair grows back, combined with the time you will need to learn new techniques, monthly photographs should enable you to detect improvements over time. Visual evidence of hair regrowth should be a potent reward for your efforts and provide encouragement for ongoing treatment commitment. For those months with minimal or no regrowth, you should take the opportunity to review the earlier exercises.

If you find yourself feeling highly uncomfortable taking photos, don't be surprised. This is a normal feeling for many hair pullers. If you find yourself overly distressed at the prospect of doing this, then don't proceed with this exercise. Many hair pullers experience extreme shame from their hair pulling and, for some, this exercise may serve to heighten their shame. It is not designed to make you feel ashamed. If you feel that uncomfortable, skip this exercise and try the next one. As we said earlier, the more tasks you undertake, the better the control you are likely to achieve over your habit. However, skipping this exercise alone will not prevent you from making strides in your hair-pulling management.

Another way to facilitate awareness and increase motivation is to enlist the support of a significant other in your treatment efforts. The fact that you are reading a self-help book suggests that you may be trying to tackle this problem without the help of a professional. For many hair pullers, there may be a dearth of professionals in their geographic area with expertise in treating this problem. For others, financial reasons, embarrassment, and prior negative treatment experiences may be additional impediments to seeking professional help. Alternatively, some hair pullers may already be pursuing psychopharmacologic approaches and wish to learn some effective behavioral tools to use in conjunction with their medications. All of these are good reasons for reading this book and they are exactly why we wrote it. In every situation, however, an actual "therapist" is missing.

While we do not feel that the presence of a therapist is absolutely necessary in every case to overcome hair pulling, it is probably more challenging to undertake this endeavor on your own. Our anecdotal experience has shown that hair pullers are likely to give up prematurely, procrastinate, or practice skills too infrequently in the absence of someone serving as a guide and support system. In fact, evidence has shown that this phenomenon occurs for medication treatment as well as for behavioral approaches.

An experienced behavior therapist can serve multiple functions including: 1) instruction in behavioral techniques for coping with urges and preventing hair pulling, 2) accountability for implementation of behavioral tools, 3) support and encouragement, and 4) assistance in problem solving when progress is absent or minimal. This is in addition to assisting you in your baseline assessment, as discussed in chapter 2. In other words, a good behavioral therapist essentially functions like a coach.

Working with a lay "coach" can also help you optimize your awareness of your hair-pulling behavior and triggers. This person can also help you practice the use of coping responses. Involvement of a significant other can also provide you with necessary support coupled with accountability.

In the next exercise, you will identify ways that a lay coach could assist you in your efforts at hair-pulling control. A coach can help you by increasing your awareness of your habit and helping you to stay committed to your treatment efforts. In addition, you could ask your coach to identify all of the situations in which he or she routinely observes you pulling your hair. You may find that your coach can identify some situations involving your hair pulling of which you were unaware.

You may decide to agree on a specified time each week when you share your monitoring record with your coach and discuss your hair-pulling episodes during the week. Alternatively, you could ask your coach to alert you any time that he or she sees you engaging in actual hair pulling, or the motor behaviors that are known to precede hair pulling for you. You may choose to share with your coach specific goals and successes in your efforts at hair-pulling management. Additionally, you can request that your coach praise you any time that he or she observes you practicing alternative strategies for hair-pulling control or hair regrowth.

Some hair pullers have also found that hairdressers, stylists, and barbers can be good resources when both sides are comfortable discussing the issue. Hair care professionals can serve in a cheerleading capacity in some cases. Since you only see them every few weeks or months, they should be able to monitor and notice progress. It will be critical, however, that they are honest in their feedback and do not shade the truth to spare your feelings.

Remember that functioning in the role of a coach can be a double-edged sword for a significant other. You will need to have an open and direct conversation with the identified person before he or she takes on this challenge. It is crucial that your coach does not become overly involved or critical during the process. It would be useful for him or her to learn about trichotillomania. We recommend that significant others read the relevant sections of this book as you are working with them so that their outcome expectations are reasonable. Of particular value for a lay "coach" will be chapter 9, "Advice for Families and Friends."

Exercise: Adding a Coach to Facilitate Awareness and Maintain Motivation

If you aren't seeing a professional therapist, or if you want to build additional support for your efforts, try to identify a family member, friend, or significant other who can adopt the role of lay "coach." You may even choose more than one "coach" to assist you! For example, Robin identified both her partner and her mother as potential coaches. She chose to share her monitoring record with her partner and asked him to gently massage her hand whenever he saw her reaching for her scalp hair. She also decided to ask her mother to positively comment if she noticed hair regrowth or if she shared with her that she had a pull-free day. Use the worksheet below to identify your coach(es) and the specific ways in which he or she can help you increase awareness and enhance motivation.

Requested Support from Coach

Coach #1: _____   1. _____

2. _____

3. _____

4. _____

5. _____

Coach #2: _____   1. _____

2. _____

3. _____

4. _____

5. _____

Maintaining Awareness and Motivation

Once you've achieved greater awareness of your hair pulling, it will be important to take steps to maintain this awareness. One effective way to do this is to continue throughout your self-help efforts with the self-monitoring as outlined in chapter 2. Another thing you can do is to complete the rating scale found in chapter 2 on a routine basis. All of these methods will provide you with updated information about your hair pulling and keep you from lapsing back into habitual, reflexive hair pulling.

Many of the techniques for maintaining awareness and motivation will keep you in touch with those compelling reasons that led you to buy this book. They will also provide you with useful information to help you flexibly adjust your hair-pulling self-help goals as you improve. Yet another strategy to maintain your motivation would be to occasionally repeat the first two exercises in this chapter, which emphasize your personal costs from your hair pulling. Now let's try one more exercise designed to heighten your awareness of your hair pulling.

Exercise: Adopting the Observer Role During Hair-Pulling Episodes

With practice, some hair pullers report that they can watch their hair-pulling behaviors almost as if they were a neutral observer. The development of this "neutral observer" can further facilitate awareness and enhance use of coping strategies while resisting urges. The next time that you are about to embark on a hair-pulling episode, try to adopt the "observer" role for yourself. Let the observer objectively note the intensity of the urges, take note of the relevant triggers, and watch how the body responds to the urges (e.g., does your hand move toward your scalp?).

You may find it useful for your self-observer to relabel the hair-pulling urges to foster greater objectivity. For example, the urges may be viewed as a short circuit in the area of the brain that controls grooming behavior. Processing the urges as "false alarms" may help to resist hair-pulling behavior in the presence of rising tension levels.

Strengthening overall awareness and developing an "observer" will take considerable time, effort, and commitment. Try it every day for the next two weeks. Rate the presence of your "observer" on a scale from 1 (very weak) to 10 (very strong).

"Observer" Ratings During Hair-Pulling Episodes

Week 1

Day 1 ____

Day 2 ____

Day 3 ____

Day 4 ____

Day 5 ____

Day 6 ____

Day 7 ____

Week 2

Day 1 ____

Day 2 ____

Day 3 ____

Day 4 ____

Day 5 ____

Day 6 ____

Day 7 ____

Once you feel confident that your motivation and awareness are heightened, it will be time for you to begin learning new strategies to prevent and interrupt your hair pulling. These coping strategies will be employed when you feel the urge to pull, think about pulling, find yourself in a "high risk" situation, or have actually begun to pull. The following chapter will instruct you in techniques for managing all of these situations.

Summary Points

► The techniques of behavior therapy are relatively simple but require practice, time, and energy to work effectively for you.

► One useful way to enhance motivation is to identify the negative consequences to hair pulling as well as the positive improvements that would occur with control over this problem.

► Identifying the motor sequence to hair pulling, using serial photographs, and objectively "observing" your hair pulling can all improve awareness.

► In some cases it can help to identify a friend or family member as a coach to offer support and guidance.

► Ongoing effort is required to maintain motivation and awareness as you continue your endeavors to achieve control over your hair pulling.

Chapter 7

Getting Behavioral Techniques to Work for You

By this point you have already done the preliminary steps of assessing your individual hair-pulling pattern and completing exercises to enhance your motivation and awareness. Now it's time to actively use behavioral strategies to better manage your hair-pulling urges and behavior. As you learn about additional behavioral tools, don't forget to continue practicing those techniques that you have already mastered. Your early techniques will provide the foundation for your self-help efforts and each new tool will be one more building block toward your success!

Use of Competing Responses

One of the cornerstone behavioral techniques for hair-pulling control is the *competing response*. The basic idea behind this technique is to replace the motor sequence of hair pulling with another behavior that utilizes the same muscle groups involved in hair pulling. Thus, the competing response is "incompatible" with hair pulling. This new behavior should be inconspicuous and not involve substituting one harmful behavior for another.

There are many different choices for competing responses. These include making a fist, grasping the steering wheel tightly while driving, or squeezing a Koosh Ball (rubber toys consisting of many string-like projections from a central core). During the competing response, the hand and muscle groups involved in hair pulling should be clenched tightly for a minimum of two minutes. The competing response provides a temporary interruption in hair pulling, during which your urges may lessen. If the competing response is sufficiently strong and is maintained long enough, there should be a sense of relief upon release of the motor behavior. At a minimum, it provides a protected time during which hair pullers can evaluate other available strategies for better control over their hair pulling.

Successful use of this technique depends on a heightened awareness of your hair pulling and your "observer" (see chapter 6) instructing you to implement your competing response. We recommend that you use this technique as soon as you are aware of any feelings, thoughts, urges, sensations, or body movements normally associated with your hair pulling. (We'd like to emphasize that sensations are an important, yet sometimes overlooked, aspect of hair pulling. Many people describe a particular scalp itch, hair texture, or oral sensation as a crucial step in the hair-pulling sequence. This is not unlike people with obsessive-compulsive disorder who have obsessions prior to compulsions, or people with tics who have sensory urges before the motor behavior.)

Use of the competing response during an actual pulling episode (known as *habit interruption*) is generally more difficult than before pulling has actively begun. Thus, it is better to use the competing response when you become aware of stroking your hair, rather than when you have already selected the hair that you wish to extract or you have already begun to hair pull.

The first few times that you practice your competing response you will probably need to time yourself with a watch or a clock to make sure that you maintain it for the full two minutes. It may seem like a long time when you first start. However, it is well worth it if it makes the difference in your ability to control your hair pulling. If you implement your competing response and the urge still remains, you should repeat the response until the urge lessens.

It is important for you to experiment with different competing responses and to choose those that work for you. You will likely have different competing responses for different situations. For example, you could grip the steering wheel with both hands while driving the car and clench your fist in response to urges while in bed at night. Jason frequently noticed that he pulled when he was involved in sedentary, quiet activities such as reading a book. He generated the following competing response options for reading and other similar situations:

Situation	Competing Responses
Reading	Hold my book tightly with both hands. Clench the arms of the chair. Hold pens or a highlighter when doing my school work.
Watching TV or movies	Grasp the arms of the couch or chair. Clench my fists.
Computer work	Hold the mouse tightly. Squeeze my Koosh Ball. Grasp the edges of my desk or chair.

Now it's your turn to do some simple exercises to make the competing response strategy a part of your treatment plan.

Exercise: Identifying Competing Responses for Your Hair-Pulling Triggers

Let's begin by having you list five situations in which you frequently hair pull. Then identify several competing response(s) for each situation.

Situation   Competing Responses

1. _____   _____

                                                  _____

                                                  _____

2. _____ | _____

_____

_____

3. _____ | _____

_____

_____

4. _____ | _____

_____

_____

5. _____ | _____

_____

_____

Now that you have mapped out competing response strategies for yourself, let's put these tools into action. The next exercise will help you to accomplish this goal.

Exercise: Monitoring Use of Your Competing Responses

For the next week, use the following sheet to record use of your competing response strategies. Make an entry to identify the situation (e.g., using the computer) each time you experience an urge. Alternatively, you may make line marks for each urge using the tic-toc method (as described in chapter 2) if you have a high frequency of urges. Then enter Y (yes) or N (no) to indicate whether you correctly implemented your suggested competing response strategies. Our clinical experience has been that those hair pullers who routinely monitor symptoms, use of techniques, and outcome are more likely to achieve desired control over their hair pulling.

In order to change the motor pattern for hair pulling, it will be important that you have sufficient awareness to use your competing responses at the appropriate times. While these exercises may seem simplistic, they will help you to get into that state of awareness, or mindfulness, that is necessary to be effective in stopping your hair pulling.

Date: _____

Situation	Used Competing Response (Y/N)
_____	_____
_____	_____
_____	_____
_____	_____
_____	_____
_____	_____
_____	_____
_____	_____
_____	_____
_____	_____

Now let's proceed to a discussion of other behavioral strategies that can also significantly reduce your hair pulling.

Stimulus Control Techniques

Another behavioral strategy that can significantly reduce hair pulling is known as *stimulus control*. This refers to modifying your environment in order to decrease opportunities to hair pull. These techniques focus on those factors that precede the actual pulling (e.g., situational variables, visual or tactile cues, etc.).

This strategy can include avoidance of situations associated with pulling (e.g., reading) or leaving trigger situations once an episode starts (e.g., going for a walk, getting a drink or snack, taking a relaxation break, or washing your face). Alternatively, stimulus control techniques can also be employed while you remain in the trigger situation. In these situations, you can limit access to hair by placing rubber fingertips (available in office supply stores) or Band-Aids over your fingers, putting a cap on your head, applying conditioner to your hair, or engaging in an activity that occupies your hands (such as knitting).

These techniques can also be used for other behaviors associated with hair pulling, such as chewing or ingesting the hair after extraction. If the sense of pleasure, relief, or gratification comes primarily from the associated oral behaviors (rather than the hair extraction) it is important to target these areas as well. In these cases, chewing gum or wearing a dental guard are stimulus control strategies that could decrease the actual hair pulling. (Note: Some of the strategies mentioned here are technically not stimulus control techniques in the strict definition of the term. However, for our purposes, it makes sense to label them in this way and to discuss them here.)

An important point is that you need to identify those strategies that will work well for you given your daily structure and lifestyle. It will not be possible for some hair pullers to totally avoid certain situations (e.g., reading a book on their syllabus for school or watching television when it is a family activity). Similarly, it will not be possible to temporarily leave other situations that can trigger hair pulling (e.g., classroom at school or staff meetings at work). Lastly, some of the strategies that impede access to your hair or interfere with ease of pulling (e.g., use of conditioner or wearing caps) may not work if you do not live or work alone. We can't emphasize enough the importance of carefully selecting your techniques when designing your individualized behavioral treatment plan.

The success or failure of this approach will also depend on the ease with which your strategies can be implemented. The amount of effort required to put the strategy into practice will be related to the likelihood of its use. For example, you may decide to use a baseball cap every time you start to pull. However, if the cap is upstairs when you experience urges, you are less likely to routinely adopt this strategy. Hair pullers should strategically place their "tools" for ready use in time of need. Now let's see what stimulus control strategies you can identify for your own use.

Exercise: Selecting Your Own Stimulus Control Strategies

Below is a comprehensive list of stimulus control techniques that other hair pullers have found beneficial. Circle those techniques that you plan to use routinely.

Strategies for any hair site:

- Wear gloves during driving or other activities
- Use rubber fingertips or Band-Aids for sedentary activities
- Apply false fingernails
- Apply hand cream or paint fingernails during sedentary activities
- Wear a blouse or shirt with tight cuffs that limit arm movement
- Put a rubber band (not too tight!) around the cuff of your shirt to limit arm movement
- Avoid reading or computer work when stressed or having urges
- Interrupt or change activity if you experience urges or pulling
- Take five minute relaxation breaks when experiencing urges or pulling
- Use a hand exerciser in situations when hands are idle
- Play with paper clips, string, textured ribbon, or floral wire
- Use a Koosh Ball, Silly Putty, a Slinky, or other hand toys, or play with a pen that has a top that can be pushed in and out
- Play with sticky Scotch tape instead of hair root
- Use your hair pulling hand for other activities (e.g., holding the phone)
- Pop bubble wrap
- Stroke or groom your pet
- Walk around the house when using a portable phone
- Choose public environments for sedentary activities (e.g., the library for working on a laptop or the family room for reading)
- Change body posture to decrease access to hair sites (e.g., sit upright in chair instead of lying down on couch)
- Sit in a different location than where you normally pull
- Eliminate hair touching and looking

Strategies for scalp hair:

- Wear a baseball cap, bandanna, or Turkish towel on your head

- Use conditioner or Vaseline in your hair

- Style hair to decrease access to preferred hairs

- Use hairspray to alter hair texture

- Wash or wet hair to alter hair texture

- Dye or tint hair to cover gray or white hairs

Strategies for eyebrows and eyelashes:

- Use Vaseline or Scotch tape on eyebrows

- Apply eye makeup that smudges with touching or pulling

- Wear false eyelashes

- Obtain professional eyebrow grooming or set regular times for eyebrow tweezing (if excessively pulling)

Strategies for oral behaviors related to hair pulling:

- Chew on alfalfa sprouts or sesame seeds (when biting on hair roots is an issue)

- Use dental guard to prevent chewing of hair

- Chew gum

- Use dental floss, self-flossers, or toothpicks

As mentioned earlier, we recommend that you obtain any necessary supplies for your stimulus control strategies (e.g., clear nail polish, hand toys, conditioner, Band-Aids, etc.) and carefully place them where you will be most likely to need them. For example, for our patients who don't mind wearing baseball caps, we have suggested that they put a cap in every location where they are likely to pull.

Now that you know how to use competing responses and stimulus control strategies to manage your hair pulling, let's discuss how you can establish your own list of hair-pulling goals.

Setting Goals

Almost everyone with chronic hair pulling wants to stop the problem behavior. Indeed, almost everyone who pulls their hair has already tried to stop, and most have been unsuccessful in their efforts. One of the most common reasons for lack of success is that hair pullers have set unrealistic goals for themselves. It is not unusual for the sufferer to try the "cold turkey" approach to treatment. This would be similar to the alcoholic who decides never to have another drink. While this may work in some cases, we have no data to show that this is a useful strategy for the average hair puller.

Another analogy would be the runner who wanted to run the Boston Marathon and set a goal of running ten miles the first day without ever having practiced before! Clearly, this is not only unrealistic, but can result in injury and a sense of failure. Feeling defeated can often interfere with future efforts to achieve behavioral goals. It would not be surprising if you have an expectation of failure while reading this book, given prior unsuccessful attempts at hair-pulling control. How then can you approach this program with confidence and hope? There are several simple guidelines that are useful to keep in mind.

First of all, it is important to set goals that are reasonable for you. What may make the most sense is for you to cut back on your hair pulling in a gradual, stepwise fashion. Your goals should be within your reach, not too hard nor too simple. One way to set goals is to focus on gradually decreasing hair-pulling frequency. Alternatively, you could set goals that address the routine use of alternative coping strategies. Presumably, if you implement useful hair- pulling control techniques, the undesired hair-pulling behavior should decrease as you increase your coping behaviors. Don't be surprised if you need to revamp your goals after you start your plan. It is not unusual for hair pullers to have difficulty knowing how hard a goal is until they actually strive to attain it.

Secondly, be sure to write down your goals soon after you embark on your behavioral plan. This keeps you honest and on track. You can always adjust your written goals if you find them too hard or too easy.

Third, remember to expect lapses along the way. No one will have a perfect treatment course. Expect to encounter pitfalls and potholes in the road! As long as you learn from your difficult times, you will be making progress even when you are struggling harder to control the hair pulling. Since chronic hair pulling is a waxing and waning problem that is reactive to many different factors, it is almost impossible to avoid snags along the way. Overall, as long as your expectations are reasonable and flexible, you should do fine with your behavioral goal setting.

Let's take a moment and go back to Jason from the introduction to this book. If you remember, his hair pulling occurred most often during quiet, physically inactive times. He established a list for himself of pull-free goals and also assigned points that he could earn according to the difficulty level of each goal. Below is Jason's list of pull-free goals and assigned point values.

Behavioral Goal	Points
Recopy history notes for fifteen minutes without pulling	1
Complete math worksheets for thirty minutes without pulling	2
Do reading assignment for thirty minutes without pulling	3
Do writing assignment for sixty minutes without pulling	5
Do reading assignment for sixty minutes without pulling	7
Write a three-to-five page history essay without pulling	10
Complete all homework for one evening without pulling	15
Complete all homework and watch TV for one evening without pulling	20

Now that we've gone over behavioral goal setting, it's your turn to tackle this important step.

Exercise: Selecting Your Own Behavioral Treatment Goals

You have the chance now to build your own goal "ladder." In this exercise you will identify successive behavioral steps that will help you to achieve your desired control over hair pulling. It is important that you generate some goals that are relatively easy, others that are medium in difficulty level, and others that will be quite challenging.

It is useful to consider your baseline profile of hair-pulling behavior as an initial starting point. This is where your self-monitoring record will come in handy. If you summarize the entries on your monitoring log, you should be able to determine an average daily frequency for your hair pulling. Also, you should be able to identify those situations most frequently associated with your hair pulling. This information will be the springboard for selecting your goals. Sample goals could include:

1. Specified reductions in the frequency of your overall daily hair pulling (e.g., 25 percent less hair pulling than at baseline)

2. Reductions or the elimination of all hair pulling in certain situations (e.g., no hair pulls while on the computer)

3. Routinely practicing hair-pulling control strategies in selected situations

Remember to be specific in describing your behavioral goals. In other words, don't write "pulling less while watching TV at night." Instead, you should write "eliminate all hair pulling while watching TV at night" or "reduce the frequency of hair pulling while watching TV by 50 percent of baseline levels." Clarity in your behavioral goals will help guide and support your efforts at hair-pulling control when you subsequently find yourself in those specified situations. In addition to specifying your goals, assign a point value for each goal according to its estimated difficulty level.

Behavioral Goal	Points

Let's summarize what you have learned so far. You have mastered the tools of competing response and stimulus control strategies. You have also set your list of behavioral goals. Now let's talk about how reward systems can promote the use of your behavioral tools to meet your behavioral goals.

Use of Reinforcement Strategies

Another common behavioral intervention is the use of *reinforcement* to help achieve desired goals. This is a relatively simple notion and it can work quite effectively if done correctly. One can systematically use rewards to increase the frequency of a desired behavior or decrease the frequency of an undesired behavior. In your case, the goal is to increase the use of alternative coping strategies and to decrease the undesired behavior of hair pulling.

According to behavioral theory, the behavior of hair pulling provides either pleasure, gratification, or relief from discomfort in those individuals who suffer from the disorder. By the time an individual wants help in controlling their hair pulling, the physical damage, negative emotional "costs" (e.g., guilt and lowered self-esteem), or the loss of desired activities (e.g., dating, swimming, etc.) have generally become unacceptable.

Let's make a comparison now using the example of eating. Eating can be emotionally satisfying (e.g., soothing, relaxing) and rewarding to our senses of taste, sight, and smell. It also provides relief from the discomfort of hunger pangs. However, when an individual overeats and gains weight, self-esteem can be lowered, physical discomfort can develop, and interpersonal relatedness can be negatively affected. At this juncture, the balance between the "benefits" and "costs" to overeating has shifted. The individual is likely to pursue professional help when the costs become more compelling than the benefits of his or her eating patterns.

When hair pulling first starts, the behavior is often low in frequency and without significant physical or emotional damage. As the habit continues the costs of the behavior increase. This balance between benefits and costs is important in determining behavioral choices. If an action has benefits and no or few costs, you are likely to select it often. If the costs increase and the benefits stay the same, the action becomes less desired. For hair pulling, the costs generally increase the longer the behavior continues, while the benefits stay the same or diminish.

Given this, you can use a reward system to increase the incentives for implementing alternative coping strategies for your hair-pulling behavior. The rewards you choose should be relative to the difficulty level of the behavioral goals. For example, in the case of Jason, it would not be appropriate to have him earn sports tickets for successfully recopying his history notes for fifteen minutes one night without hair pulling. The difficulty level reported for this behavioral goal was low (i.e., point value = 1) and, thus, a relatively minor reward should be available for accomplishing this task or he should be required to successfully complete this goal for several nights before earning a reward.

Let's review a potential reward system for Jason. Jason pulled almost every day, generally during sedentary activities like using the computer, reading, and watching TV. Jason has been practicing competing responses and the use of stimulus control techniques with his therapist. He loves baseball, collects baseball cards, and enjoys receiving baseball caps for the different teams. He wants a Starter jacket from the Boston Red Sox, his hometown team. He would like to see the Red Sox play with his best friend, and he wants to go to the Baseball Hall of Fame.

The first step we took was to establish a hierarchy of rewards for desired behaviors and identify a point value for each reward. It looked like this:

Reward	Point Value
Stay up fifteen minutes past bedtime during the school week to watch a baseball game	5
Stay up thirty minutes past bedtime during the school week to watch a baseball game	15
Pack of baseball cards	25
Stay up late on a weekend night to watch an entire game	50
Baseball cap from desired team	75
Videotapes of classic baseball highlights	100
Tickets to the Red Sox with friend	150
Red Sox Starter jacket	200
Trip to the Baseball Hall of Fame	500

Now that you've learned about the basics of reward systems, let's try an exercise that will help you to establish your own reward strategy.

Exercise: Selecting Your Own Reward System

Identify items or activities that you could use in your own reward system. Remember: Choose items that you have access to but which currently are not freely available. Your system will not work unless you are willing to withhold these rewards until you achieve your goals. Establish point values according to the cost or importance of each reward. You should have a range of rewards and point values so that you can earn some rewards fairly soon and most of your rewards within a few weeks if you are working diligently on your behavioral treatment plan.

Suggested Reward(s)	Point Value

Terrific! Now you're ready to actually implement your reward strategy for improved hair-pulling control.

If you find that your reward system is not working effectively, either your goals are too high or the rewards are insufficient for the difficulty level of your goals. It's important to emphasize that a reward system should not be started until you've learned alternative strategies for managing your urges and trigger situations. Behavioral research has repeatedly shown that it is ineffective to make efforts to decrease a behavior without substituting more functional alternative behavior. By this point, though, you should be routinely using the competing response and stimulus control techniques and these should help you to significantly decrease your hair pulling.

Now let's shift our focus to discuss another strategy that can similarly help you reach your behavioral goals. This technique, like reinforcement strategies, also involves the implementation of specific consequences as a function of your behavior.

Use of Additional Consequences

Another similar behavior therapy technique is known as *punishment*. When we use the term "punishment" in this book, we use it differently than the lay public. There is no implication that you, or any other hair puller, are "bad" or "lazy" because you pull out your hair, and thus you deserve or need to be punished. In this circumstance, punishment is used as an incentive to avoid a behavior, but is not a statement about your worthiness as a person. Our intention is simply to present one more method to help you use coping strategies rather than engage in hair pulling.

The principle underlying the concept of punishment is also very basic. Behaviors that have negative consequences (rather than rewards) are more easily extinguished than those behaviors that do not have similar consequences. Thus, although hair pulling is associated with bald patches or hair thinning in the long run (which may be experienced by the hair puller as punishing), in the short run the person may experience a sense of relief, or even pleasure, which immediately reinforces and strengthens the behavior. If hair pulling continues, the presumption is that the immediate positive outcomes outweigh the long-term negative outcomes of hair loss or lowered self-esteem. The goal with punishment strategies is to program more immediate negative consequences that can outweigh the immediate positive consequences of an unwanted behavior.

Punishment techniques can take many different forms. A simple and mild form of punishment, which does not appeal to everyone, is to snap a rubber band around the wrist each time a hair is pulled. As with other behavioral therapy techniques discussed above, the success of this technique depends upon practiced awareness, a strong "observer," and a willingness to implement these tools. To be effective, this negative consequence must be applied immediately, on a regular basis, after any hair is pulled.

Another punishment strategy, which is often preferred by many hair pullers, is called *response cost*. This refers to the loss of something positive whenever the undesired behavior occurs. For example, the hair puller can forfeit pleasurable activities (e.g., playing computer games, watching videos, etc.) when hair pulling occurs. For this to be effective, it must involve "discretionary" activities that the hair puller has control over and can terminate at will.

You could implement response cost in one of two ways. First, you could agree to terminate specific pleasurable activities if hair pulling occurs during the activity. For example, you could decide that you turn off your television set for a half-hour period any time that you extract one hair. Alternatively, you could decide to lose points whenever you hair pull. In this latter scenario, you would lose the privilege of desired activities (e.g., eating out, purchasing a new sweater) when you have accumulated an excess negative point count.

When using the latter response cost strategy, you would first identify desired activities or items that you would be willing to forfeit. Then an assigned negative point value will be established both for the undesired hair-pulling behaviors as well as the positive activity or item that will be lost. For example, you could assign a negative point count of 50 toward eating out every Saturday night. Similarly, you could establish a negative point value of 10 for every hair-pulling episode that occurs while watching TV. If you accumulated 50 negative points, you would forfeit going out to eat the following Saturday night. As we did for the reward system, you should construct two step ladders. One ladder would list undesired hair-pulling behaviors. The other ladder would specify positive activities that could be forfeited (i.e., punishments) as a result of hair-pulling behaviors. Every step of each ladder should have a negative point value assigned. The point value should be commensurate with the severity of the hair-pulling behavior or the value of the activity to be forfeited.

Remember Sally from the introduction to this book? Sally had already learned some hair-pulling control techniques. She wanted to use response cost strategies, in addition to these tools, to decrease both her hair pulling in bed in the morning and her high frequency hair-pulling binges. As an example, Sally first wrote out her step ladder of undesired hair-pulling behaviors with their associated negative point values.

Undesired Hair-Pulling Behaviors	Negative Point Value
Pull five hairs in bed upon arising, without eating any of the roots	-5
Pull five hairs in bed upon arising, and eat some or all of the roots	-10
Pull ten hairs in bed upon arising, without eating any of the roots	-15
Pull ten hairs in bed upon arising, and eat some but not all of the roots	-20
Pull ten hairs in bed upon arising, and eat all the roots	-25
Pull twenty-five hairs in bed upon arising, and eat some but not all of the roots	-35
Pull twenty-five hairs in bed upon arising, and eat all the roots	-40
Pull fifty or more hairs in less than an hour and eat some of the roots	-50
Pull fifty or more hairs in less than an hour and eat all of the roots	-60
Pull one hundred or more hairs in one or two hours and eat some of the roots	-70
Pull one hundred or more hairs in one or two hours and eat all of the roots	-80

Next, Sally identified her step ladder of possible response cost items (i.e., activities or items to be forfeited) and their associated negative point values.

Response Cost Items	Negative Point Value
Forfeit TV while getting dressed in the A.M.	-5
Forfeit using special perfume in the A.M.	-15

Forfeit ice cream after lunch	-20
Forfeit morning newspaper break	-25
Forfeit a long bubble bath in the evening	-35
Forfeit one hour of pleasure reading before bed	-50
Forfeit a ten-minute long-distance phone call to a good friend	-60
Forfeit all television for the day	-70
Forfeit getting a special video from the store	-85

Once Sally completed both of her step ladders for a response cost approach, she was ready to effectively use this approach to control her hair pulling. The first day that she started to use this approach she pulled ten hairs in bed and ate all of the roots, and she later had a binge of greater than one hundred hairs and ate some of those roots. Her negative point values for the two activities, 25 and 70, respectively, totaled 95 negative points. From her list of punishments, she chose to forfeit her evening bubble bath and a ten-minute long-distance call. By the next day, Sally was even more committed to using her competing response and stimulus control strategies that she had learned earlier.

By this point you may be wondering whether it is best to use reinforcement or punishment strategies, or a combination of both. There is no universal wisdom to guide you in this decision. What we generally advise against, however, is the use of punishment strategies alone in the absence of rewards for more functional behavior. Some hair pullers choose to exclusively use reinforcement strategies. Other hair pullers combine reward and punishment strategies in an effort to optimize their hair-pulling control. We can't emphasize enough that this is an individual decision. You need to know yourself well enough to be aware of how much time and effort you are willing to invest in your behavioral plan. It may be overwhelming to start with both reinforcement and punishment techniques at the same time. If you choose to use both approaches, we would suggest that you start with one strategy and add on the other only when you have mastered the first.

It would not be surprising if you have strong feelings about the use of punishment versus reinforcement strategies. This is certainly understandable. Some of you may have been punished when you were younger for pulling out your hair. As stated earlier in this section, punishment strategies should never be used with the idea that the hair puller deserves punishment because they have this problem. Quite the contrary! It should only be used with the understanding that it is a behavioral strategy that can help to motivate sufferers to control their hair pulling once they have mastered effective alternative coping strategies.

Exercise: Designing Your Own Response Cost Strategy

If you choose to implement response cost strategies, you should complete the worksheets below. (If not, skip to the next section entitled "Relaxation and Breathing Techniques.") First you will need to identify the undesired hair-pulling behaviors.

Undesired Hair-Pulling Behaviors	Negative Point Value
	- _____
	- _____
	- _____
	- _____
	- _____
	- _____
	- _____
	- _____
	- _____
	- _____

The next step would be to list positive activities that you are willing to forfeit (i.e., punishments) if you accumulate the specified number of negative points. Now identify those punishments and assign appropriate negative point values.

Response Cost	Negative Point Value
_____	- _____
_____	- _____
_____	- _____
_____	- _____
_____	- _____
_____	- _____
_____	- _____
_____	- _____
_____	- _____
_____	- _____
_____	- _____

So far you have mastered the behavioral tools of competing response and stimulus control, you have constructed your own behavioral goals, and you have identified how reinforcement and punishment strategies can help you meet your goals. Now let's shift gears and discuss some relaxation techniques. These tools may be useful for hair pullers in two ways. One, you can employ them proactively to reduce stress that may trigger your hair pulling. Secondly, you may find them beneficial for coping with any discomfort that you experience when you are actively resisting hair-pulling urges.

Relaxation and Breathing Techniques

You may find on occasion that the use of competing responses, stimulus control, and reinforcement and punishment strategies are insufficient for the control of your hair-pulling behavior. In these instances it may be the case that your stress levels are quite high and you need additional skills for coping with external stressors or the discomfort you experience when trying to resist hair pulling.

In these instances relaxation and breathing exercises may be particularly helpful, especially for those individuals who experience the sensations and symptoms of anxiety (e.g., stomach upset, restlessness, muscle aches). As always with behavioral techniques, practice is crucial, and relaxation exercises should be done at least twice a day when you are starting out. In the beginning, the best thing is to practice your relaxation under nonstressful conditions. Once you have mastered these relaxation techniques, they should be used in conjunction with other behavioral tools for better control over hair pulling.

There are many diverse strategies you can use to master relaxation skills. Some involve the practice of actual muscle tensing and relaxing, while others focus on your mental processes. We generally recommend muscle relaxation protocols since some of these steps mimic competing responses (e.g., tensing and relaxing the hands). In addition, physically-focused relaxation practices more likely provide a better distraction from hair-pulling urges than sedentary techniques (such as imagery). Following is a sample muscle relaxation protocol for you to practice.

Before you start your practice, however, first make sure that your environment is comfortable and free of distractions. You may want to disconnect the phone and turn off the lights. Begin by lying on your back with your arms and legs uncrossed. Tense your toes for ten to fifteen seconds, then release them for about the same length of time. Gradually work your way up through your body, tensing and releasing each of your muscle groups. Repeat the tensing and relaxing sequence for your calves, thighs, hands, lower arms, buttocks, abdomen, upper arms, chest and back, shoulders, and neck. Lastly, tense and relax your mouth, nose and cheeks, eyes, and forehead. Once you have completed the sequence, lie still for a little while and try to sustain the feelings of relaxation. If any tension returns to any of the muscle groups, focus on that area and try to release the tension.

Exercise: Record of Your Relaxation Practices

For the next week, practice your muscle relaxation exercises once or twice a day and use the chart that follows to record your success. Make an entry for the date, time, and duration of each practice. Then rate your relaxation levels before and after practice on a scale of 1 to 10, with 1 being extremely relaxed (about to fall asleep) and 10 being extremely tense (feeling like you could jump out of your skin from tension).

Date	Time	Duration of Practice	Relaxation Level	
			Before	After
————	————	————————————	————————	————————
————	————	————————————	————————	————————
————	————	————————————	————————	————————
————	————	————————————	————————	————————
————	————	————————————	————————	————————
————	————	————————————	————————	————————
————	————	————————————	————————	————————
————	————	————————————	————————	————————
————	————	————————————	————————	————————
————	————	————————————	————————	————————

Once you have mastered this form of muscle relaxation, you can move on to imagery and breathing strategies.

Imagery techniques generally involve focusing on a pleasant scene. The scene can be a memory of a relaxing vacation or a scene that you conjure up in your imagination. Common examples include the beach on a hot sultry day, a mountaintop vista, snuggling in bed on a winter night, taking a nap in a hammock, or sitting by a stream. Whatever scene you select, it is important that you try to experience it with all of your senses. For example, for a beach scene, see the distant blue of the horizon, smell the ocean water, and hear the waves lapping on the shore. Feel the hot grains of sand between your toes, taste the salt in the air, and experience the warmth of the sun as it beats down on your exposed skin. Ask yourself what else you notice about your scene. You may wish to add to the image a picture of yourself with your hair styled as you would like to wear it.

Some people find it easier to visualize scenes than others. Some people are better at using one or another sense (vision, hearing, touch, smell, taste) in their imagery. For other individuals, imagery exercises may be tedious and frustrating. If you don't find it helpful, put your emphasis on practicing the earlier relaxation strategy or a diaphragmatic breathing technique.

Diaphragmatic breathing is another strategy for controlling stress and inducing relaxation. The goal with this technique is to use your diaphragm muscles to breathe rather than your chest muscles. Using your diaphragm may also slow down your breathing rate if you are a rapid breather. Now try to picture a baby breathing in a crib. When the baby inhales, watch the stomach expand. Watch the stomach deflate when the baby exhales. This breathing sequence is more conducive to relaxation than chest breathing, which is what most people have become acculturated to practicing.

Now let's try diaphragmatic breathing. Keep your breathing at a comfortable, slow pace, inhaling through your nose and exhaling through your mouth. Put a hand on your abdomen to check that your diaphragm (which is actually the sheath of muscles between the bottom of your lungs and your stomach) expands when you breathe in. While your chest will also expand a little when you inhale, your diaphragm should expand substantially more. Think of the word "relax," and silently say "re" as you breathe in, and "lax" as you breathe out.

Now that you have been introduced to a few different relaxation strategies, it's time for you to practice them until they are second nature. It's up to you to decide which form of relaxation to practice. You can use the same chart to record your practices of imagery and breathing techniques that we used earlier for relaxation practices. Over time, you'll probably find that you will develop your own relaxation protocol that will include some combination of progressive muscle relaxation, diaphragmatic breathing, and imagery.

We find that hair pullers who do these relaxation exercises are more successful in managing their hair pulling. Relaxation techniques may be effective for several reasons. Clearly they provide alternative, functional ways for coping with stress. Equally important, though, may be the fact that they enhance your state of awareness, which is critical for the use of coping techniques.

Our next section will review the potential role that your thoughts may play in your hair pulling. Then we will discuss cognitive techniques you can use to change your thoughts and control your hair pulling.

Cognitive Strategies

As discussed in chapter 5, cognitive interventions for chronic hair pulling are based on models that view thoughts, emotions, and behaviors as interrelated. According to these models, how one thinks can directly affect one's behavior, or indirectly affect behavior through how one feels. In a reciprocal fashion, one's behavior will similarly impact one's thoughts and feelings. Let's apply these concepts to the problem of hair pulling and look at some examples to illustrate these points.

Sally can pull hundreds of hairs on a bad day. Sally views herself as having a weak character because she is unable to control her problem. She is aware of the negative internal dialogues, or "tapes," that constantly play in her head. These include thoughts such as:

- "You're a weak person and you can't control your hair pulling."

- "You can pull out those white hairs because everyone else does that too."

- "You might as well pull out those hairs that are bothering you because if you resist now you'll just pull them out later."

- "You won't be able to complete writing your report for work without pulling out some hairs."

- "It's okay to pull some hairs from the right side of your scalp so that it matches the left side where you pulled hairs last night."

- "You can pull just one hair and then you'll stop pulling after that."

- "One hair doesn't matter. Most people lose more hair than that with brushing and shampooing their hair."

- "You pulled out some hairs the last time you studied for a chemistry test, so you probably will do a lot of hair pulling tonight. The coping tools you've been using probably won't be strong enough to handle this situation."

Having each of these thoughts increases the probability that Sally will engage in hair pulling. Some of these maladaptive thoughts directly allow her to pull hair (e.g., "I can pull just one hair and then stop"). Other cognitions encourage hair pulling by labeling the situation as challenging and Sally as having limited coping abilities (e.g., "I can't cope without pulling," or "Pulling will make me less anxious").

As discussed in chapter 5, several psychologists have written about the role that one's thoughts can have in one's hair pulling. Vicki Gluhoski (1995), in her cognitive model, suggests that maladaptive thoughts can initiate, mediate, or worsen hair pulling. She maintains that three categories of entrenched beliefs exist that can be related to hair pulling. These are beliefs about the value of hair pulling, permission-giving beliefs, and automatic thoughts about a situation that produces negative emotions.

Now it's your turn to identify your unique thoughts related to your hair pulling. Remember: It's not unusual for these thoughts to be overlearned and deeply ingrained, requiring considerable effort to bring them to the surface.

Exercise: Identification of Your Negative Thoughts Related to Hair Pulling

Take a moment now to list all the thoughts that come to mind that are likely to trigger, allow, or worsen your hair pulling. It should take some time and effort before you are able to identify most of them. You may want to jot some down initially, put the list down, and then come back to it at a later date. At this point we only want you to list your hair-pulling thoughts (without evaluating them).

Your Maladaptive Thoughts Related to Hair Pulling

1. _____

_____

2. _____

_____

3. _____

_____

4. _____

_____

5. _____

_____

6. _____

_____

7. _____

_____

8. _____

_____

9. _____

_____

10. _____

_____

Once you have identified your maladaptive thoughts, the next step is to restructure these thoughts. The goal is to change these thoughts so that they are adaptive and supportive. Some people mistakenly understand this approach and replace their original thoughts with unrealistic, "Pollyanna-like" thoughts. This is not the goal of this exercise! If the new thought is not rational and believable, this strategy won't work.

There are a few questions that can be of use when trying to challenge and restructure your maladaptive thoughts. You could ask yourself the following eight questions:

- What is the evidence for this thought?

- What is the evidence against this thought?

- What is another way that I can look at this situation?

- How else could other people look at this situation?

- How would I respond to a friend if he or she had this thought?

- What is the worst thing that can happen?

- Am I using all-or-nothing thinking?

- Is this thought based on feelings rather than fact?

(Aaron Beck and his colleagues have outlined a number of cognitive errors that are commonplace in maladaptive thoughts. David Burns [1980] in his bestselling book, *Feeling Good: The New Mood Therapy* catalogued ten distinct forms of cognitive distortions. You may wish to consult this book to understand more about the specific errors in thinking that you could be making. Identification of these errors could also help you to generate more positive and adaptive replacement thoughts.)

Let's now illustrate these principles with an example. Sally's last maladaptive thought was "You pulled out some hairs the last time you studied for a chemistry test, so you probably will pull out a lot of hairs tonight. The coping tools you've been using probably won't be strong enough to deal with this situation." Sally asked herself the eight suggested questions and realized that she was predicting that she would once again have the same urges and succumb to them by pulling out her hair. She realized that she could use what she learned from her past experience and develop a plan for coping with this situation without pulling. She realized that a more adaptive substitute thought for her would be: "Even though last time you pulled some hairs while studying your chemistry, now you have some behavioral tools that will help you cope with your urges to pull. You can use your competing response to control urges, take breaks, practice relaxation if stressed, and offer yourself a reward for managing your pulling better. Being prepared for this situation will help you to successfully handle it differently than you did the last time."

Now let's go back to your list of maladaptive thoughts and generate more effective substitutes for these thoughts.

Exercise: Restructuring Your Maladaptive Thoughts

From your list of maladaptive thoughts in the last exercise, copy all your entries onto the left side of the following worksheet. Then generate substitute adaptive thoughts for each entry using the list of suggested questions for help in restructuring thoughts.

Maladaptive Thought	Restructured Thought
1. _____	1. _____
_____	_____
2. _____	2. _____
_____	_____
3. _____	3. _____
_____	_____
4. _____	4. _____
_____	_____
5. _____	5. _____
_____	_____

6. _____   6. _____

_____   _____

7. _____   7. _____

_____   _____

8. _____   8. _____

_____   _____

9. _____   9. _____

_____   _____

10. _____   10. _____

_____   _____

You have now learned a wide array of cognitive behavioral coping tools that will help you to more effectively deal with hair-pulling events. It will be important for you to remember your tools, practice them, and prepare in advance for challenging situations.

Relapse Prevention

We have discussed earlier that your goals for hair-pulling treatment should be realistic and that lapses should be expected in your course of recovery. It is not uncommon for behavior therapy techniques to have a dramatic effect in the beginning. Similarly, it is not unusual for hair pulling to increase at a later point, possibly in the context of a new stress or, alternatively, due to declining awareness or motivation. When this occurs, it is important that you do not give up and get discouraged, but instead continue with your treatment efforts.

You will need to remember the difference between a "lapse" and a "relapse." In the former, symptoms increase temporarily. The latter refers to a loss of all gains and a return to baseline levels of functioning. Once you have learned behavioral skills, it is our feeling that you will never return to the starting gate if you continue to use your techniques, even if your hair-pulling frequency temporarily increases. Remember that these lapses are simply an expected part of your treatment. As therapy progresses, there should be fewer and fewer lapses.

It is also critical that you make an effort to limit how far you fall back when you encounter a lapse. Keep the hair pulling to a minimum and do "damage control" to reduce the hair loss as much as possible. The less you go off track, the easier you will find it to return to your treatment plan. Make a note of all the techniques that you have successfully used in the past and make a renewed effort to use them again to your benefit. The more you use your techniques, the more practiced and accomplished you will be in fighting your hair-pulling urges. Don't forget to frequently review your coping strategies and to use your assessment tools (both self-monitoring and the self-report scale) to evaluate your status on an ongoing basis.

In summary, setbacks are expected but every effort should be made to control them and get back on track. If you keep working on your cognitive behavioral techniques, you will ultimately break through any lapses or impasses that you encounter. The main point is to continue your efforts at all times to move forward!

Summary Points

▸ Many cognitive behavioral tools are available for the management of hair pulling. Among these are competing responses, stimulus control techniques, goal setting, reinforcement and punishment strategies, stress management tools, and cognitive interventions.

▸ The individual hair puller needs to select tools that he or she is willing to implement routinely. Successful use of these strategies requires considerable time, effort, and practice.

▸ Stress can play a significant role in the triggering and exacerbation of hair-pulling urges. Stress management techniques are important, especially for hair pullers who tend to experience physical symptoms of anxiety.

▸ Cognitive techniques focus on the role of maladaptive thoughts in hair-pulling behavior. Identification and correction of these thoughts can be a useful tool in hair-pulling control.

▸ Lapses are expected in the course of hair-pulling treatment. It is crucial that you try not to be discouraged by lapses when they occur. Focus on limiting the hair loss and resume treatment efforts as soon as possible.

Chapter 8

Other Kinds of Help

Psychological treatment and medications are not the only kinds of help available, and psychologists and psychiatrists are not the only people who can offer help. In this chapter we will discuss the other sources of help available for hair pulling. Much of this help comes from consumer organizations founded by sufferers to help others with the same problem. In this chapter we will also discuss a number of general questions, such as how to go about finding a mental health professional who can assess and treat your hair pulling.

Consumer Organizations

There is one organization in the United States, the Trichotillomania Learning Center (TLC), that is dedicated exclusively to individuals with trichotillomania and related disorders. Also of interest to many with trichotillomania is the Obsessive Compulsive Foundation (OCF). Both of these groups have affiliates or support groups in many areas of the United States. At the end of this chapter there is information on how to contact these organizations.

The TLC is an international not-for-profit educational organization supported by memberships. It was founded in 1991 by a trichotillomania sufferer to provide information on both the experience of, and the treatment for, trichotillomania and related body-focused disorders. The TLC membership packet is the most comprehensive public information packet available on this disorder. TLC publishes a newsletter (called *In Touch*) and also sponsors an annual retreat, conferences, symposia, talks, and other events. It maintains a database of experienced clinicians to provide referrals for treatment. It also provides much needed networking resources around the world for sufferers, family members, and professionals. TLC works to develop and maintain support groups nationally and internationally, and keeps a database of contacts for these groups. It has been a powerful force in bringing together interested clinicians and researchers and in developing alliances with other organizations for the benefit of its membership and the public.

The OCF is also an international not-for-profit organization that was founded in 1986 for people with obsessive-compulsive disorder, their families and friends, and interested professionals. This organization may also provide some limited information on trichotillomania. The OCF publishes a bimonthly newsletter and is a clearinghouse for a selection of books, articles, and tapes on OCD and related disorders. It maintains a database of clinicians experienced in the treatment of these disorders and assists individuals with treatment referrals. It supports the development of local support groups (and refers sufferers to these groups) and assists OCF affiliates around the country and abroad. The OCF has an annual three-day conference that is open to patients, families, and professionals alike. They sponsor a Behavior Therapy Institute (BTI) that trains mental health professionals in the use of behavior therapy techniques. The OCF has been successful in educating the public about OCD and in obtaining financial support to fund research projects on OCD.

We strongly recommend that people with hair pulling and their loved ones join the TLC (and the OCF if interested) to learn more about trichotillomania. The newsletters of these consumer organizations are particularly helpful insofar as they provide information about the latest research and give readers a sense of support in their fight against hair pulling. Connections with other sufferers through these organizations, local support groups, and newsletters can be extremely useful in breaking the sense of isolation and reducing the shame that many hair pullers experience.

Internet Virtual Groups

The Internet has heralded a new avenue of help for hair pullers in the form of virtual support groups. There now exist several different bulletin boards and chat rooms devoted specifically to either trichotillomania or OCD. Members of these support groups communicate with one another using electronic mail (e-mail). (E-mail is part of the standard package of resources that all Internet service providers give their customers, and it's increasingly available throughout the world.)

Subscribers to a particular mailing list can communicate by sending e-mail messages to a specific computer server, which then automatically distributes these messages to all subscribers on this list. Every message is given a header by the sender (e.g., "Serotonin in trichotillomania"), so that a series of messages, or a virtual conversation, develops around a number of themes or issues.

Many Internet groups have been developed exclusively for trichotillomania. It is important, however, that you approach the Internet and mailing lists with some caution. Mailing lists may differ in the extent to which they include the participation of professionals and the provision of accurate information. In some cases there is no censorship of the information that is presented. Other problems with mailing lists include those that might be experienced in any social activity or group, including personality clashes among different subscribers. While these virtual forums may provide information and support to some sufferers, others feel that this format does not work for them.

Dietary Approaches to Treatment

A view that has some popularity in the trichotillomania community is that dietary approaches may be helpful for hair pulling. One such diet recommends the elimination of specific food items including sugar, caffeine, eggs, legumes, nuts, and soy products.

It is well known that certain foods can worsen particular psychological disorders. For example, in people with panic disorder, excess amounts of caffeine are known to precipitate panic attacks. In addition, it is also believed that certain nutritional components can be helpful for specific disorders. Along these lines, there is some evidence that particular fish oils may be helpful in bipolar disorder and high doses of inositol may be useful for certain mood and anxiety disorders.

However, although particular diets often seem promising for psychiatric disorders, when rigorously studied they have often been found ineffective (such as the sugar-free diets for attention deficit disorder). To our knowledge, the diet described above for hair pulling has not been published in the scientific literature and has not been subject to careful research. Therefore, we cannot recommend it positively due to its lack of empirical support. We have no quarrel, however, with those who would like to try it in addition to using more well-studied treatments.

Finding a Mental Health Professional

For many hair pullers, it can be a difficult task trying to locate a professional with the necessary training and experience to help them. Many medical professionals still lack basic knowledge about the disorder and are unfamiliar with the treatments that can be of help. In fact, many professionals continue to label hair pulling as OCD, even though we now know that it is different in many ways.

Before you start on your journey to identify a treating professional for yourself, it's important to recognize the distinctions between different mental health practitioners. Different kinds of professionals offer unique skills and services. Thus, determining the kinds of skills and services that you require may be a useful first step toward finding the appropriate professional for you.

For example, psychiatrists are medical doctors who go on after their basic medical training to specialize in the discipline of psychiatry. Psychiatrists can have particular skills in diagnostic assessment (not only of hair pulling but also of other emotional problems), in prescribing medication (psychopharmacology), and, sometimes, in psychotherapy. A psychiatrist would be a good choice if you feel that your hair pulling is accompanied by other emotional problems, if you suffer from a medical disorder, or if you wish to explore the option of medication.

Psychologists usually complete a doctoral degree in psychology and, subsequently, a clinical internship in their area of specialization. Psychologists can specialize in psychotherapy, psychological assessment, or research. Many psychologists specialize in a particular school of psychotherapy, such as cognitive behavioral or psychodynamic psychotherapy. A psychologist who is trained in cognitive behavioral psychotherapy would be a good choice if you prefer to try nonmedication approaches to control your problem. If you have additional psychological or emotional problems, other adjunctive psychotherapy may also be of value. Social workers may also specialize in the treatment of psychological disorders and may do psychotherapy. Nurses, as well, may be trained in the prescription of medication, psychotherapy, or both.

Despite the differences between the various mental health professionals, a specific interest in, and knowledge of, hair pulling may ultimately be the most important factor in choosing a practitioner. After all, psychiatrists frequently refer patients for psychotherapy to psychologists, while psychologists and social workers frequently refer patients to psychiatrists for medication consultations. Unfortunately, there are relatively few practitioners in general that focus on hair pulling exclusively in their clinical practice.

So how do you track down professionals in your geographic region? There are several ways you can go about this task. As an initial step, we recommend that you contact the TLC to access their database of professionals who specialize in this disorder. Similarly, the OCF maintains a database of mental health professionals who treat OCD and related conditions. (It is not uncommon for professionals who treat hair pulling to also specialize in the treatment of OCD.)

Another approach is to contact the local professional board or association for the specific type of mental health practitioner (e.g., psychology, psychiatry, social work) that you are seeking. Additionally, some professional associations are organized around a specific treatment orientation or specialty of those practitioners. For example, the Association for the Advancement of Behavior Therapy (AABT) consists of a professional membership who primarily utilize cognitive behavioral treatment approaches (their contact information is at the end of this chapter). Lastly, contacting members of a local support group can also help you identify those local professionals who treat hair pulling. This last approach can also provide you with a consumer evaluation of the specific treating practitioner.

Once you have identified some professionals in your area, your next task is to evaluate the specific individual and decide whether you wish to pursue treatment with him or her. How do you go about doing this? You will want to assess these clinicians in two areas: 1) their overall competency as mental health professionals and 2) their specific expertise in trichotillomania. In general, any mental health professional should listen to your concerns, be empathic, and interact with you in a respectful way. You should feel that these professionals exhibit some flexibility in their approach and are open to those treatment avenues that are necessary for you to get better. To evaluate their specific experience and competency in treating trichotillomania, you could ask them the following questions.

- Do you specialize in the treatment of trichotillomania or OCD?

- How many patients have you treated with trichotillomania?

- What psychological treatments or medication approaches (depending on their discipline) do you recommend?

- What is your therapeutic orientation?

- How have your patients responded to your treatment?

- What do you feel are reasonable expectations for treatment outcome with this disorder?

For psychotherapists, we recommend those individuals who describe themselves as cognitive behavioral in orientation. They should describe the frontline treatment as including habit reversal techniques. In general, we recommend the use of treatment techniques and medication approaches that have been shown to be effective through research studies. While professionals who treat patients with OCD may be more comfortable with trichotillomania than general mental health practitioners, they may still not be aware of the specifics of treatment that are unique to hair pulling. If there is a lack of professionals in your area who have experience with trichotillomania, we recommend you search for someone who is willing to learn more about this problem (through reading or other resources) while he or she is treating you. We caution you to be wary of any professionals who say they can "cure" you and indicate that your problem can be effectively treated in only a few sessions.

Dealing with Hairdressers

Many people with hair pulling avoid visits to hairdressers out of embarrassment over their symptoms. In many cases, however, the hairdresser can be an important ally in your fight against hair pulling. This can happen in one of several ways. If the hairdresser is aware of your pulling, he or she can serve as a coach and a support system to help you control the pulling. Additionally, most men and women agree that looking good helps them to feel good. In many cases when a talented hairdresser can successfully style your hair to look good despite thinning or bald patches, you can feel some renewed hope and attempt to break the hair-pulling cycle to limit further damage.

There are two possible strategies in dealing with your hairdresser. The first is to be totally open about your hair pulling. This approach is not for everyone! You have no obligation to disclose this information if you do not feel fully comfortable doing so. If you have known your hairdresser for some time, you are probably better able to assess what his or her reaction will be to your disclosure. If you are in doubt, you can always hold off on telling your hairdresser until a time in the future when you feel more comfortable doing so. If you prefer not to tell your hairdresser that you suffer from trichotillomania, you can honestly say (if asked) that you have a medical condition that results in hair loss.

Wigs and Hairpieces

Many people with hair pulling consider using wigs and hairpieces to cover bald patches. In some cases, we think that this is a reasonable strategy. Once again, it has to be acknowledged that for many people looking good is an important part of feeling good. A wig or hairpiece can be important in helping to fight the shame and embarrassment that are so often a part of trichotillomania.

Also, in some cases, wearing a wig or hairpiece can limit pulling due to limited access to the scalp. However, in other cases, we have had patients who have started pulling hair from their wigs! From a purely behavioral point of view, wearing a wig or hairpiece can also be an avoidance behavior that ultimately worsens symptoms. When one has the ability to hide the consequences of repeated pulling episodes, the incentive for controlling urges and resisting pulling can be less. Thus, it is often important to practice not wearing them for some time each day. Every effort should be made not to pull out hair at these times. It may be useful to gradually increase the amount of time the wig or hairpiece is not worn each day.

Friends and Family (To Tell or Not to Tell)

Many people with hair pulling hide their symptoms from friends and family. This may be associated with feelings of shame and embarrassment and with having to avoid various social situations. Others make no attempt to hide their hair loss, but then suffer rude stares, impertinent questions, or unwanted advice from strangers. What is the best route to take?

One of our patients, Jenny, had known her boyfriend, Robert, for about five years before they decided to marry. During this time he had not once seen the bald spot on the crown of her head. She always made sure to cover this up with her long hair or with a scarf. In addition, she made sure to restrict her hair pulling to those times that she used the bathroom. Robert's one complaint was that she spent an inordinate amount of time in the bathroom.

As Jenny and Robert's wedding date got closer and closer, she began to increasingly feel like she was deceiving him. Would he love her and marry her if he really knew what she was doing in the bathroom? On the other hand, if she continued to pull her hair in secret, then this would mean that he really did not know her and that their relationship was ultimately incomplete. It was this quandary that ultimately led Jenny to seek treatment.

Each person has to decide for himself or herself what he or she is willing to let any particular friend or family member know. The decision is often quite complex. You need to weigh things out for yourself. You may find it useful to write down a list of advantages and disadvantages of disclosing your hair pulling.

It is not necessary to tell the whole truth to everyone. Certainly, many people with medical disorders do not discuss their illness with everyone that they meet. Particularly when relationships are still at an early or superficial stage, we feel that focusing on hair pulling as a problem can lead to particular relationship biases. For example, such a focus may act to keep the hair puller in the patient role and the acquaintance in the helper role.

No one should be ashamed and embarrassed about hair pulling. Once again, people with medical conditions are entitled to receive the support and care of loved ones. No one would think of blaming a person if he or she were to develop a lung infection. On the contrary, there is a duty to help such a person. Similarly, people with hair pulling deserve the support and assistance of their loved ones.

Summary Points

▶ Support in the fight against hair pulling can be obtained from a number of sources. Consumer organizations, especially TLC, can be helpful in both education and treatment referrals.

▶ Virtual support groups may also provide information and empathy.

▶ In some cases, telling a hairdresser may be useful in soliciting support and tips on how best to style your hair.

▶ Hairpieces and wigs can be useful in some cases by limiting access to pulling and by making you feel better about your appearance if this is an issue for you. In other cases, however, they may allow you to pull freely knowing that the physical damage can be hidden, and thus interfere with the positive effects of treatment.

▶ There is no need to feel ashamed or embarrassed about hair pulling. However, it is also not necessary to tell everyone the entire truth about your problem.

▶ The following information can help you get in touch with supportive organizations:

  1. Trichotillomania Learning Center
     1215 Mission Street, Suite 2
     Santa Cruz, CA   95060
     Phone: 831-457-1004
     Fax: 831-426-4383
     E-mail: trichster@aol.com
     Website: www.trich.org

  2. Obsessive Compulsive Foundation, Inc.
     337 Notch Hill Road
     North Branford, CT   06471
     Phone: 203-315-2190
     Fax: 203-315-2196
     E-mail: info@ocfoundation.org
     Website: www.ocfoundation.org

  3. Association for the Advancement of Behavior Therapy
     305 Seventh Avenue, 16th Floor
     New York, NY 10001
     Phone: 212-647-1890
     Fax: 212-647-1865
     Website: www.aabt.org

Chapter 9

Advice for Families and Friends

Trichotillomania can have a significant impact on the family and friends of the sufferer as well as on the individual hair puller. At times, it can be just as hard to watch a loved one suffer (and feel helpless to improve his or her situation) as it is to live with the problem itself. This chapter is largely devoted to those issues facing family and friends when they are aware that someone they love is hair pulling.

Until recently, there have been few sources of help or accurate information for loved ones. Misunderstanding and ignorance still exist in the medical community as well as in the general public. The lack of good educational materials makes it hard for loved ones to learn more. The existence of many myths makes it hard for hair pullers to easily disclose their problem. It is crucial, however, that friends and family members educate themselves about the disorder, as the reactions of loved ones can have a significant impact on the sufferer.

Unfortunately, in some cases, family and friends may be aware that a loved one is experiencing psychological distress or avoiding certain activities, but be unaware that hair pulling is the cause. Many individuals will not disclose their problem out of fear that others will think they are crazy or react in shock or disgust. The dissemination of simple facts, such as the statistic that at least one to two in every one hundred individuals hair pull, would go far to make the problem seem less abnormal. In turn, this would make sufferers feel less alone and much more willing to be candid with family and friends.

In those situations where significant others are aware that a loved one is pulling, they may be unsure of the best ways to provide support. They may fear saying or doing the wrong thing and upsetting the sufferer and making the pulling worse. Some may decide to consciously ignore the behavior, believing that this shows respect for the puller's privacy. Unfortunately, inaction can sometimes leave the puller feeling more isolated and neglected. By doing this, significant others may also limit their outlets for the expression of feelings about their loved one's problem. There are actions that family and friends can and should take to help their loved one as well as themselves in coping with this problem.

When individuals minimize their hair pulling, family and friends may feel especially unsure about whether to push on the issue or back off. In such situations, we recommend that significant others take the following steps. One, you should try to locate educational materials on this disorder and recommend that the sufferer learn about the illness (perhaps giving him or her a copy of this book). Two, you should indicate a willingness to help and offer hope for success in controlling the problem. Three, you should identify support groups and other avenues through which the sufferer can be in contact with other hair pullers. If these interventions are not successful in getting the individual to accept the problem, we recommend that you do not force the issue. You may then seek help for yourself, if necessary, to better cope with how the problem of you friend or family member affects you.

Alternatively, family and friends can be the ones who minimize or deny the problem. This can sometimes occur when parents feel that they are "responsible" for their child's problems. They can mistakenly assume that the hair pulling is attributable to their genes or inadequate parenting, trying to avoid feeling guilty by not recognizing the problem. If the cosmetic damage is hidden or appears minimal, trichotillomania may seem like a minor bad habit to friends and family. It can be difficult to understand the impact of the illness, especially since it is often disproportionate to the amount of actual hair loss. In these cases, pullers can feel that their issue is not being taken seriously and have negative feelings about the lack of help.

If you have, up to this point, been minimizing the problem, it may be time to communicate directly with your loved ones about the illness and its impact. It often is necessary for sufferers to help educate significant individuals in their life so that they will be better equipped to understand and provide support. It may be useful for you to attend a conference or presentation on this topic. Alternatively, your loved one might request you to accompany him or her to a visit with a professional to discuss the illness, or to read this book and receive help and support with the exercises contained in it.

On the opposite end of the scale, some family and friends can be too quick to suggest solutions. Family and friends can often feel responsible for fixing the problems of their loved ones. They can become frustrated if they can't find the "answers" or the problem does not quickly resolve. Conflict and tension may then develop if significant others feel that the puller does not routinely use their suggestions or other strategies. In these cases it is important for you to follow the lead of your loved one, allowing him or her to decide if there are any concrete strategies that you can employ to help with his or her hair pulling. It's up to the hair puller to let you know how you can help. It's up to you to respect the hair puller's wishes regarding what is or isn't helpful to him or her.

Now we will discuss some of the common misconceptions about hair pulling, as well as the reality of the disorder. Then we will review some general guidelines on how to support and interact with loved ones who pull out their hair. For the most part, these sections apply when both the sufferer and the loved ones are aware of the problem and there is some communication between them about it.

Myths About Hair Pulling

It is not unusual for myths to develop about psychological problems, especially when scientific information is sparse. Hair pulling has been particularly susceptible to this phenomenon given the relative recency of research interest in this field. Furthermore, health professionals have had limited success in educating the public about this disorder. Following are some of the commonly held myths about this disorder and the actual truths about the illness.

Myth #1: Hair pulling is "just a bad habit" and does not have serious consequences.

Historically, many disorders such as hair pulling, nail biting, and thumb sucking were labeled as "bad habits" by professionals. At that time, caregivers lacked the knowledge about these problems that we have today. Unfortunately, it is likely the case that many hair pullers still experience responses from others that reflect this outdated perspective on the disorder.

These problems have been commonly thought to be a sign of nervousness or stress. In truth, there are many theories, but we still do not know exactly what causes people to engage in these behaviors. Stress can be involved, but it is likely only one of many factors that may be involved in the problem.

Hair pulling is far from being "just a bad habit." The consequences to this disorder are far-reaching and can affect most aspects of the hair puller's life. As discussed in earlier chapters, hair pulling can be accompanied by serious psychological and medical problems. Included among these are depression, anxiety, shame, lowered self-esteem, localized infections, scarring of the hair follicle, dental erosion, carpal tunnel syndrome, gastric complications, and even death (from trichobezoars, which are intestinal hairballs resulting from ingested hair). Furthermore, hair pullers can be seriously limited in their choices of leisure, social, and occupational activities as a function of their hair pulling.

Myth #2: Hair pulling is a sign of serious mental illness and reflects deep-seated emotional problems.

Historically, mental health professionals believed that the behavior of pulling out one's hair was the surface manifestation of serious underlying psychological conflicts. There has been no research data to substantiate this notion.

Of course, it may be the case that some individuals who have serious psychological problems also pull out their hair. However, there is no reason to believe that all hair pullers have such problems or that these problems are the source of their hair pulling. In fact, some of the psychological symptoms reported by hair pullers, such as depression, can be the result, rather than the cause, of their hair pulling. A significant proportion of hair pullers are high-functioning individuals who do not exhibit other serious psychological issues.

Myth #3: Hair pulling is a sign of weakness or neurosis.

This is one of the most harmful myths that many people have about hair pulling. Underlying it is the notion that hair pullers can stop if they *really* wanted to do so. Additionally, some falsely believe that those who continue to pull out their hair are just lazy or weak in character. There is absolutely no evidence to support this idea! Whatever else it is, hair pulling is not merely a failure in willpower.

On the contrary, many hair pullers are highly accomplished individuals. Many have successfully addressed other emotional problems (such as addictions or eating disorders) but find it hard to control their hair pulling. Our clinical experience working with hundreds of sufferers suggests that the majority of our patients have been highly motivated to address their hair pulling. Unfortunately, though, hair pulling can be a highly challenging problem to treat.

Myth #4: Hair pulling is always a sign of a disturbed childhood.

This myth stems from older psychodynamic theories that attribute most psychological issues to problems during childhood. As discussed in chapter 3, there is little hard data to corroborate this notion. Oftentimes it has been questioned whether early traumatic experiences (especially sexual or physical abuse) could be the triggering event. While undoubtedly there are hair pullers who report abuse and other childhood stressors, we have no reason to think that this is always the cause of hair pulling.

These ideas can be quite harmful as they place responsibility for the problem solely on the parents of the hair puller. It can be hard enough for parents to watch their children suffer with the physical and emotional consequences of their hair pulling habit without being blamed as the cause of it.

Myth #5: Hair pulling is only a problem when there is visible hair loss.

One of the more surprising research findings is the limited association between the extent of physical damage and the severity of its psychological impact. We have worked with many individuals where their visible hair loss is minimal, yet the damage to their self-esteem has been profound. Clearly, variables beyond the extent of hair loss are involved in determining the psychological consequences to this problem.

What Not to Say to People with Hair Pulling

Most hair pullers have heard one or more of the following comments from others who have known about their problem:

- "We all have bad habits . . . it's just a bad habit."

- "No one else I know does that. What's wrong with you?"

- "It's just another phase you're going through."

- "Do you still do that? I thought you had outgrown that."

- "Stop feeling sorry for yourself. Just get over it."

- "You need to calm down. It's just stress."

- "Why can't you just pull yourself together and stop it?"

- "What's wrong with you? Why do you keep doing that?"

- "Don't you have any willpower?"

- "Do you realize what you're doing to yourself?"

- "Why would you want to harm yourself?"

- "Don't you care about your physical appearance?"

- "You know how much this upsets me. Why do you still do it?"

- "Are you doing this just to spite me?"

- "If you listened to the doctor, you'd be better by now."

- "I'm disappointed in you. You had been doing so well."

- "You looked so pretty when your hair grew back. Now you look awful again."

- "I don't understand it. You had stopped the hair pulling and now you're doing it again."

Needless to say, these comments are unlikely to help the sufferer or promote good will between the hair puller and those around them. The most likely outcome to these reactions is to emotionally shut down sufferers so that they are less likely to open up in the future about their problem. Additionally, it may have the added effect of worsening their shame and (already) lowered self-esteem.

What to Say to People with Hair Pulling

There is no universal set of guidelines on how to respond to someone who suffers with this problem. Every hair puller's struggle is unique and they will have different preferences as to how significant others should relate to them around their problem. Some hair pullers eagerly welcome daily involvement and frequent support from those in their lives. Others, however, prefer to address their hair pulling more on their own with the knowledge that others support them and their struggle.

It is only through direct communication between the sufferer and significant others that it becomes clear what role family and friends can adopt to provide support and assistance. For this to occur, the sufferer needs to be aware of how he or she would like others to be involved. They also need to communicate this directly, as others cannot be expected to be mind readers. Family and friends should be receptive and recognize that the best way to help is by listening and respecting the requests of the puller.

Many significant others expect themselves to solve the problems of those they love. This is an impossible task. It is the responsibility of the sufferer to address their problem, though family and friends can play a major role in providing support, increasing awareness, and reinforcing use of behavioral techniques. Below are some general guidelines as to how you can best interact with your loved one around the issue of his or her hair pulling.

Offer Unconditional Support and Acceptance

Hair pullers already commonly feel a lot of shame, lowered self-esteem, and isolation as a result of their hair pulling. They are already suffering tremendously because they have this disorder and other people don't. Most sufferers are very reluctant to disclose their problem out of fear that others will react badly. A critical response from family or friends can be emotionally scarring and cause them to retreat once again into isolation. Family and friends need to be careful not to blame the victim. Blaming the person with the problem serves no useful purpose for anyone.

It is critical that sufferers know that their family and friends will love them despite having this problem. They should not be afraid that they will lose the love of a partner or the approval of a parent if they pull. This would only add more stress to their life and may make them more likely to engage in the problem behavior! Tell your loved one that you love him or her regardless of how successful he or she is on controlling the hair pulling.

We all have problems of our own that we expect our partners to accept and learn to live with. The sooner you can adopt this same stance for the hair pulling, the sooner you will be helping your loved one as well as yourself. It is important that you accept, but not resign yourself, to your loved one's hair pulling.

Knowing that significant others' feelings are not contingent on their success in controlling the hair pulling can help them have the strength to persevere during challenging periods. It is important for significant others to convey that hair pullers aren't failures if they are pulling, as long as they are trying their best to manage their problem. While you may not always be able to impact the actual hair pulling itself, you can always affect your loved one's self-esteem by how you interact around this issue.

Ask Your Loved One to Help You Understand More About Their Problem

It is not unusual for family and friends to try to understand the plight of hair pullers by making an analogy to other problems they themselves have experienced. This is risky business! Don't assume that you know what your loved one is going through.

Hair pulling can be a very complicated and challenging problem, and it can even present quite differently in different individuals. There are no simple solutions to this problem. Don't make the mistake of putting your own feelings and thoughts into the head of the hair puller.

One of the best ways that you can show support is to *ask* hair pullers how you can better educate yourself about this problem. Ask them to tell you more about the details of their problem. Ask them if there is anything that you can read to help you learn more about their condition. It is a sign to sufferers that you care when you want to learn more about what they are going through.

Ask Your Loved One How You Can Help Them with Their Hair Pulling

Very often family and friends want to solve the problems of those they love. They may expect themselves to know the answers to the problems of those they care about. While the intention is admirable, unfortunately, it is not within your ability to find the solution for your loved one. First of all, there are still many answers that even the researchers in the field do not have about this disorder. Secondly, only the individual sufferer knows the specific details of their problem, which are critical for identifying successful tools and techniques.

As stated earlier in this chapter, sufferers differ widely regarding how they want significant others involved in their efforts to control their problem. What you can do is openly express your desire to help and listen to what the hair puller suggests. Encourage direct and open communication about the problem to the extent that the hair puller is comfortable with this. Be sure, however, not to pressure pullers to prematurely reveal details of their hair pulling that they are not yet comfortable disclosing.

It is the responsibility and privilege of sufferers to map out their own treatment plan and to determine the involvement of family and friends. Sometimes they themselves are not sure what coping strategies will work. Provide them with the space to consider different alternatives and be there to help implement and evaluate these strategies.

Offer Encouragement for Small Steps and Support When Setbacks Occur

Many family and friends view hair pulling as a simple, concrete problem that should have an easy solution. Unfortunately, they can make the mistake of expecting overnight success and improvement without any lapses along the way. Very often it takes time to find the right tools and techniques to manage hair-pulling urges and behavior. The fact that it takes time to control the hair pulling does not necessarily reflect in any way on the motivation or efforts of the sufferer.

Furthermore, the disorder is known to be waxing and waning in its course and highly reactive to stress. Thus, it is likely that there will be setbacks along the path to better management of the problem. This does not have to be devastating. The important thing is to learn what is possible from these setbacks and for pullers to get back on their path to better management of their symptoms.

Don't be inflexible in your efforts to assist hair pullers. If you insist that hair pullers employ specific interventions when they feel unable to do so, you run the risk of alienating them. They may then fear that they have let you down and avoid seeking out your assistance in the future.

One of the most important roles that family and friends can play is to offer reinforcement for small, steady steps toward progress. You can facilitate this by being a coach and cheerleader (see the exercise in chapter 6 designed for this purpose). Your loved one will go through a process that results in the successive acquisition of new tools to manage urges and control the behavior. Your support can encourage his or her sustained effort and practice. We suggest that you focus more on reinforcing the use of coping strategies than reductions in actual hair pulling, because hair pullers generally have more control over the former than the latter.

You should expect and embrace lapses as learning experiences that can offer useful information about the sufferer's disorder. It is important that you are flexible and that you verbalize reasonable expectations. Make every effort to be nonjudgmental with lapses, as pullers often feel disappointed and discouraged by their inability to resist their urges. Use humor as a coping technique to the extent that it helps the sufferer maintain objectivity regarding their problem and is not perceived as minimizing their suffering.

Following is a checklist designed to help you identify optimal ways to interact with the hair puller around this problem. The questionnaire is for friends and family, so you can assess your current behavior and emotional responses to the problem.

Exercise: Checklist for Friends and Family

	Yes	No
Have you asked the hair puller how you can learn more about the problem?	____	____
Have you expressed your desire to offer help and emotional support?	____	____
Have you followed through with any requests for assistance made by the sufferer?	____	____

Have you been reasonable in your expectations for the puller regarding the problem?   ____   ____

Have you been reasonable in your expectations for yourself regarding this problem?   ____   ____

Have you been able to avoid expressing disappointment, anger, or criticism when the hair puller is unable to control the pulling?   ____   ____

Have you been able to avoid responding to the hair pulling in a humiliating or demeaning fashion?   ____   ____

Have you been able to avoid bringing attention to the pulling in a public setting?   ____   ____

Have you offered support when the sufferer made small steps toward progress?   ____   ____

Have you expressed a willingness to talk when the puller seemed upset over the hair pulling?   ____   ____

Have you offered to be in the physical proximity of the puller or engage in a distracting activity when he or she is having a difficult time?   ____   ____

Have you expressed to the hair puller that your love and friendship are not related to his or her success in managing the hair pulling?   ____   ____

Have you tried to keep the hair pulling in perspective in your relationship with the sufferer?   ____   ____

Have you addressed any other issues in your relationship with the hair puller that may impact his or her hair-pulling problem?   ____   ____

Summary Points

- ➤ Hair pulling can have a significant impact on families and friends as well as the individual sufferer.

- ➤ Significant others should not assume they understand what the hair puller is going through or how best to treat it.

➤ Every hair puller is different and will have different preferences regarding the involvement of others.

➤ Hair pullers should directly communicate to others how they can be supportive and help control the hair pulling.

➤ Above all, it is important that significant others communicate acceptance and support regardless of their loved one's success in controlling the hair pulling.

Chapter 10

Children with Hair Pulling

Hair pulling in children can vary a great deal from child to child. The pattern of your child's pulling and the causes of his or her behavior can be quite different from that of another child with hair pulling. Children with hair pulling can also differ according to their stage of cognitive and emotional development, as well as their corresponding skill levels. Furthermore, children will vary as to whether they view their hair pulling as a problem and are motivated to seek treatment. In summary, successful treatment of your child will require a comprehensive and sophisticated assessment of his or her hair pulling coupled with an individualized treatment plan.

Very Early Onset Hair Pulling

While the average age of onset for hair pulling is typically twelve or thirteen years, hair pulling can begin at almost any time. In fact, hair pulling has been reported in children as early as the first year of life. It is difficult, however, to estimate how many children pull out their hair in their younger years. This is because, in some cases, the hair pulling occurs for only a short period of time. In other cases, when it lasts for many years, there may be relatively long periods of remission.

It has been suggested that childhood hair pulling can be divided into two different types according to age of onset (Swedo et al. 1992). The first type, occasionally called "baby trich," occurs in children of preschool age and is viewed as similar to a benign habit. "Baby trichs" are made up of equal numbers of boys and girls, or perhaps even more boys than girls.

In very young children, hair pulling may function to self-soothe. It is unlikely that the typical pattern of tension or anxiety beforehand, and relief afterward, plays a major role for these hair pullers. There is unfortunately not much research on very young hair pullers and the course of hair pulling in this group over time. Clinicians have suggested that when hair pulling begins in preschoolers, the children usually outgrow it. If you are the parent of a child with "baby trich," while it is certainly worth obtaining a professional consultation, it is probably likely that this is a temporary behavior that will disappear with time.

Later Onset Hair Pulling

The second type of hair pulling in children begins in adolescence and is the focus of most of this book. Hair pulling in adolescents and adults may differ from that seen in the young preschool child in a number of ways. In particular, it seems more likely to become an entrenched habit that persists over time. It may also be more likely to be accompanied by other psychological problems. Hair pulling in older children may have a negative impact on various aspects of development, for example, affecting self-esteem and interfering with relationships. Accordingly, specific treatment interventions need to be designed for such children. As for adults, the first part of the treatment process with child hair pullers is a comprehensive assessment.

Assessment of Children

Assessment of hair pulling in your child will require a different approach than in an adult. As indicated earlier, very young children will lack the insight and cognitive maturity necessary for adequate analysis of their hair pulling. For example, preschool children may be unable to identify common situations and feelings that accompany their hair pulling. Additionally, they will be unable to keep self-monitoring logs or complete self-report questionnaires of hair pulling behavior. Therefore, in the very young hair puller, parental figures become the primary source of information during the evaluation process.

As children mature, they increasingly become better able to play a key role in both assessment and treatment. This may take the form of recording the occurrence of the problem behavior and associated variables. Alternatively, it could be putting into action some simple, concrete treatment interventions.

The majority of the assessment literature has focused on the adult hair puller. There are no self-report hair-pulling instruments designed specifically for children or adolescents, and there are no standard self-monitoring records consistently used by all treating professionals with this age group. As a result, treating professionals will need to tailor their assessment tools according to the cognitive maturity level of the individual child.

To develop an effective behavioral treatment plan, it will be necessary to identify all of the relevant triggers for the hair pulling. In the case of the preschool child, it is important to identify associated situations and sensory aspects of the hair pulling. As the child gets older, emotions and cognitive beliefs related to the hair pulling also become important to assess. As discussed in earlier chapters, successful treatment will require identification of those factors that are unique to each individual hair puller.

To summarize, below is a list of factors that are important to consider prior to the development of a treatment plan for a child or adolescent:

- Age of the child

- Emotional and cognitive maturity of the child

- Level of knowledge regarding hair pulling

- Triggers to hair pulling (e.g., situations, moods, thoughts, sensory cues)

- Consequences to hair pulling (e.g., change in mood, sensory feedback, thoughts, responses from others)

- Associated "habits" (e.g., thumb sucking, nail biting)

- Associated psychological problems (e.g., depression, anxiety, attention deficit, tics)

- Social, academic, and leisure consequences to hair pulling

- Motivation for treatment (both child and family)

- Emotional readiness for treatment (both child and family)

- Treatments beliefs/expectations (both child and family)

- Prior treatment experiences or home remedies

- Family dynamics (e.g., issues of control, attention, autonomy, conflict)

- Access to services

- Ability to afford treatment

Causes of Childhood Hair Pulling

Several different hypotheses have been put forth to account for the origins and maintenance of childhood hair pulling. Among these are streptococcal infections, dysregulation of the neurotransmitter serotonin, genetic inheritance, modeling of the behavior by others, high levels of stress, and certain parenting styles that may impact hair-pulling behavior. These factors are discussed at length in chapter 3 of this book.

It is possible that the causes of hair pulling often involve many different variables. A *diathesis-stress model* may be a useful way to think of the origins of this disorder. This model suggests that hair pullers may have a predisposition to the illness, which later becomes activated by stress. In some cases, the predisposition may be genetically transmitted. The specific stress could involve a psychosocial event (such as loss, death, or geographical relocation) or a medical event (such as a streptococcal infection). Subsequently the hair pulling may be self-reinforcing or externally reinforced by the environment.

There is no current agreement among professionals as to the predominant cause(s) of this problem in children. There is some limited data to suggest a role for each of these variables. Therefore, until we have conducted considerably more research in this area, it would be premature to emphasize one hypothesis over another.

Treatments for Children

Due to a lack of treatment studies for child hair pullers, there are no established standards of care for this age group. In general, though, there is a consensus to emphasize behavioral approaches over medications when treating children. Medications are most often used to treat child hair pullers when other psychiatric conditions are present or after behavioral approaches have been unsuccessful. Traditional psychotherapy, while possibly helpful in addressing issues of self-esteem and family conflict, hasn't been shown to effectively decrease the hair pulling itself.

Several important variables are different between the preschooler and older child. Due to the developmental and cognitive immaturity of the young child, we believe the involvement of the parent or another authority figure is always necessary. The very young hair puller will lack the ability to self-monitor, to understand what triggers the hair pulling, and to systematically use treatment strategies. Therefore, in the preschool hair puller, important figures in the child's environment play critical roles in both accurately assessing the problem and consistently implementing treatment steps.

With preschool children, behavioral strategies may include engaging the child in activities incompatible with hair pulling at high risk times for hair pulling. For example, if a child is prone to hair pull when watching television, it may be useful to encourage him or her to use a hand toy during these times. If sensory factors appear important, it will be necessary to identify alternative ways to obtain similar sensory stimulation. Thus, if children are soothed by tactile contact with their hair, they may be encouraged to rub a piece of material or play with string or ribbon. Gentle prompts and reminders may be necessary if, and when, the child hair pulls.

Decreasing the amount of time that the child is alone or limiting sedentary activities may significantly reduce the amount of hair pulling. The systematic use of rewards, including praise and food treats, may be used. However, when using rewards it is important to set reasonable behavioral goals according to the child's age and the severity of hair pulling. It is always important to recommend a different, substitute activity (such as playing with Silly Putty or a Koosh Ball) when providing rewards for preventing or limiting an unwanted behavior. In addition, rewards with children should immediately follow success due to their difficulty in delaying gratification.

Several studies of young children have reported an association between hair pulling and other "habits" such as nail biting and thumb sucking. In several cases, treatment of thumb sucking alone has been successful in the elimination of the hair pulling. One of the techniques used has been the application of an aversive tasting substance to the thumb. Another has been to use a thumb post, a device constructed of polypropytene which, when attached to the thumb, limits flexibility (Watson and Allen 1993).

As child hair pullers grow older, they become better able to take more responsibility for their treatment. Several other developmental issues, however, become relevant and require careful consideration in mapping out a treatment plan. During adolescence many individuals (not just hair pullers!) engage in conflict with their parents around issues of control and autonomy. Often, by the time professional treatment is sought, parental figures have made numerous attempts to beg, bribe, or nag his or her child into stopping their hair pulling. If you are a parent, we would recommend that you not use these strategies with your child. Not only are these attempts generally unsuccessful, but they often create negative feelings between the child and the parents around the hair pulling and its management.

Furthermore, age-related reluctance to disclose concerns about appearance or difficulties with self-control of unwanted behavior may present added treatment challenges. Particularly with the adolescent hair puller, it is important that the child is emotionally willing and prepared to begin treatment. Adolescents may be reluctant to involve their parents in treatment. This can occur if they feel that their parents' expectations for improvement are unreasonable or if they perceive their parents as controlling or critical.

With early school age children and adolescents, most case studies in the literature attempt to use modified versions of habit reversal (also known as habit control training). Varying levels of success have been reported with these approaches in individual case studies and case series. Further studies with larger samples of hair pullers are sorely needed to document the success of these treatment techniques and evaluate their long-term outcome. For older children and adolescents, we strongly recommend the self-help workbook entitled *The Hair Pulling Habit and You*, written by Ruth Golomb and Sherrie Vavrichek (1999).

Advice for Parents

Having a child who hair pulls can present numerous challenges to a concerned and loving parent. For most parents, watching their child engage in an abnormal behavior, as well as observing visible balding or hair thinning, can result in considerable heartache. Even worse can be the recognition of the toll it takes on your child's emotions, self-esteem, and peer relationships.

To start with, many parents have to address their own fears that they are responsible for their child's affliction. Since their child inherited their genes, and they are responsible for their child's upbringing, many parents conclude that it must be their fault if their child hair pulls. Furthermore, since they are the parents, they often mistakenly conclude that it is their responsibility to find solutions to the problem.

Neither of these conclusions is necessarily correct. To date, our knowledge of the role of genetics in this disorder is quite limited. We also have no reason to conclude that faulty upbringing is the culprit. Furthermore, it is unreasonable to expect yourself to have "the answers," especially since the professionals themselves often feel limited in their ability to help some hair pullers. Especially when the hair puller is an adolescent, it is primarily the hair puller's responsibility to understand and manage his or her own problem.

The following case study illustrates some of the challenges confronting the parents of a child with hair pulling, as well as some of the possible solutions.

Susie, an eight-year-old girl, was brought by her mother to see a psychologist to deal with her hair pulling. Susie's mother had first noted some mild hair loss on the top of Susie's scalp while brushing Susie's hair two years ago. To her mother's concern, the hair loss had expanded rapidly over the past several months. Susie now had an area of scalp two inches in diameter that was almost completely bald.

Susie's mother brought her to the family physician who completed an examination and some lab tests. The physician reported that Susie did not appear to have anything visibly wrong with her hair and her scalp had not appeared inflamed. A quick lab test on one of her hairs failed to reveal a fungal infection. Blood tests did not suggest anything wrong with her general health. The physician then reviewed some possible reasons for hair loss, mentioning that some children pull out hair. He asked Susie's mother whether this could be the case with Susie. Susie's mother said she had never observed this and couldn't believe that her daughter would do such a thing! Susie quietly denied that she was pulling out her hair. Her physician then referred her to a local dermatologist.

The dermatologist also did not find anything obviously wrong with Susie's scalp or hair. He also asked whether Susie pulled out her hair. Susie's mother became quite upset that a second doctor would suggest that her daughter might pull out hair. She vehemently said that this wasn't the case and asked what else could be done. The dermatologist suggested a biopsy of the scalp area that was affected. Although Susie protested, her mother insisted on the procedure.

Two weeks later Susie and her mother returned to the dermatologist. The dermatologist somewhat cautiously broke the news that the biopsy revealed a pattern of hair and scalp changes that was consistent with trichotillomania. Although her mother was shocked at the diagnosis, Susie finally admitted to pulling out her hair. The dermatologist suggested a lotion that would decrease any itching in the affected scalp area and calmed the mother by saying that hair pulling in children was usually short-lived and would probably resolve on its own.

On the way home from the dermatologist, Susie's mother asked Susie why she hadn't told the truth before and why she pulled out her hair. She told her that she absolutely must stop pulling. Later that day, as Susie's mother calmed down, she realized that she had been harsh on her daughter. She vowed to do everything she could to help Susie stop pulling out her hair.

Over the next few months, Susie's mother vigilantly monitored her daughter's behavior. She soon realized that Susie had probably been pulling out hair in her presence all along. Susie's mother recalled being very preoccupied with Susie's grandmother's failing health at the time Susie first demonstrated hair loss. She realized that during that period she had been spending less time with Susie and giving her less attention than usual.

She then focused more and more of her attention on Susie's behavior, reminding Susie not to pull out hair when hair pulling was observed. Her reminders began as gentle prompts but, as time went on, she found herself more and more frustrated with Susie when her hair did not grow back. At times she caught herself yelling at Susie to stop pulling, or telling her that if she really wanted to stop she could. At that time, this was something that she firmly believed. At times she even punished Susie, for example by turning off the TV if Susie was pulling out hair while watching the television. She became embarrassed to take Susie out and spent more time styling Susie's hair.

Susie's hair pulling at times appeared to get better, only to worsen shortly thereafter. It became obvious that Susie was frustrated not only with her hair pulling but also with the multiple corrective interactions with her mother. The mother-daughter relationship then began to center around hair pulling and little else. Susie's mother then began to note that Susie even appeared to pull out hair to spite her at times, as if communicating "I will do what I want to, you can't stop me." After two years of frustration, Susie's mother began to think that if she shaved Susie's head, she might stop the behavior long enough so that she could get control over it. She went to see if the psychologist thought that this was a good idea or whether there were other options.

The psychologist listened to Susie's mother's story and collected more specific information about Susie's hair pulling and moods from both Susie and her mother (who were seen together and then separately). After a complete analysis, the psychologist concluded that Susie was too young and too ambivalent about her hair pulling to use habit reversal, the behavioral procedure most useful for adults. Although Susie desired a full head of hair, the psychologist also recognized that hair pulling in many ways had become a double-edged sword. Although Susie was bothered by and ashamed of her hair pulling, it was a way for her to assert her independence and sense of control. The hair pulling also brought her parental attention, albeit counterproductive attention, which she had missed out on earlier.

The psychologist advised the mother against shaving Susie's head, as this often brings on more shame and embarrassment. Additionally, Susie would likely start pulling again when her hair grew back. She also suggested that the mother become less invested in controlling Susie's hair pulling and let Susie take more responsibility for recovery. She advised that it could take some time before Susie really developed the motivation to change. However, she said there were techniques and principles that Susie's mother could use to assist Susie in the meantime.

Over the next few sessions, the psychologist, Susie, and her mother identified activities that Susie enjoyed that would keep her hands occupied at times when she normally pulled out hair. The first activity they chose was rug hooking. They also developed a program to reward Susie for success in not pulling our hair, rather than punish her for pulling out hair. Suzie earned a star every day that she didn't pull out hair. Accumulated stars could be redeemed for something Susie requested, in this case, Barbie dolls and accessories.

Susie's mother was also instructed to ignore Susie when she was pulling out hair (other than to take a mental note that this was a hair-pulling day) and to spend more time with Susie when she wasn't seen pulling out hair. She was advised to praise Susie on how beautiful her hair was and to offer additional praise at the end of each week if hair appeared to be growing in. Susie's mother was also encouraged to reinforce any progress on the rug-hooking project.

Over the course of several months both Susie and her mother were able to change their approaches. Although Susie occasionally still pulled her hair for attention, she soon became self-motivated to not pull out her hair. She was enjoying the projects that kept her hands busy and seemed pleased with her mother's praise and rewards for not pulling. Eventually the hair growth itself became a strong reward and motivated her further to not pull out hair. As time passed, Susie and her mother found their relationship growing closer with fewer and fewer discussions centered around hair pulling.

So what can you do if your child is a hair puller? Here are a few suggestions and guidelines to help you cope with this difficult situation. To start with, it is important to accept that your child is a hair puller, though not resign yourself to it. This is a subtle but important distinction. Avoid blaming yourself for your child's suffering or for the lack of existing solutions. Recognize that your role may be more to support than control your child. Make every effort to listen to your child and provide unconditional acceptance. Your love and approval should not be based on whether or not your child hair pulls, but rather on who your child is as an individual. Make every effort to emphasize accomplishments and give your child perspective on the disorder.

Try to convey to children that while they may pull out their hair, this behavior does not define them as an individual. It may be useful here to think for a moment about similarities and dissimilarities between hair pulling and nail biting. Both are repetitive motor behaviors that are nonfunctional and can cause damage to one's physical appearance. Both are viewed as "habits" that may be difficult to stop. Yet it is interesting that many people would find it considerably more upsetting when children pull out their hair than when they bite their nails.

Perhaps we are more eager to control hair pulling than nail biting because hair is viewed by most as being so central to one's physical appearance. It would rarely, if ever, be the case that nail biting would be considered a major problem or a defining characteristic for a child. One might argue that, from this perspective, it is unfortunate that hair pulling is so often identified as such a significant problem. By saying this, however, we do not mean to minimize the impact that this problem can have. Rather, it is our intention to help provide some perspective and context for the problem.

In some situations, children may be fearful of telling their parents about their problem with hair pulling. If you notice that your child has bald patches or hair thinning, don't hesitate to tell him or her what you have observed. Mention to them that you are aware that hair loss can occur from pulling out one's hair. Express concern over your child's psychological and physical well-being. Communicate a desire to listen and support. It is often useful to get more information about the problem and offer to identify and engage professional help.

Above all, it is essential that children know that they are not alone. Identification of a local child support group—or an Internet peer buddy, bulletin board, chat room, or support group—can be invaluable. For further discussion on how to help your child, consult chapter 9. Also, don't hesitate to find professional help for your child, as therapists can assist you in developing an individualized treatment program.

Summary Points

▸ Hair pulling in children can vary considerably in onset, causes, symptom picture, and prognosis.

▸ Professionals lack consensus regarding the causes of childhood hair pulling, though it is likely multifactorial in origin.

▸ Assessment approaches and treatment strategies differ according to the age and maturity level of the child hair puller.

▸ No standards of care exist for treatment of the child hair puller, though most professionals emphasize behavioral approaches over medication when treating children.

▸ Parents of child hair pullers should not blame themselves for their child's problem nor expect to find the "answers" to the problem without the help of a professional and the cooperation of their child (especially adolescents).

References

American Psychiatric Association. 1994. *Diagnostic and Statistical Manual of Mental Disorders*, Fourth Edition. Washington, D.C.: American Psychiatric Association.

Azrin, N. H., and R. G. Nunn. 1977. *Habit Control in a Day.* New York: Simon and Schuster.

Bhatia, M. S., P. K. Singhal, V. Rastogi, N. K. Dhar, V. R. Nigam, and S. B. Taneja. 1991. "Clinical profile of trichotillomania." *Journal of Indian Medical Association* 89:137–139.

Burns, D. D. 1980. *Feeling Good. The New Mood Therapy.* New York: William Morrow and Company.

Christenson, G. A., S. J. Crow, T. B. Mackenzie, R. D. Crosby, and J. E. Mitchell. 1994. "Placebo controlled double blind study of naltrexone for trichotillomania" (abstract), *New Research Program and Abstracts of the 150th Annual Meeting of the American Psychiatric Association.* Philadelphia, Penn.: NR597.

Christenson G. A, S. L. Ristvedt, and T. B. Mackenzie. 1993. "Identification of trichotillomania cue profiles." *Behavior Research and Therapy* 31:315–320.

Christenson, G. A., T. B. Mackenzie, and J. E. Mitchell. 1991. "Characteristics of 60 adult chronic hair pullers." *American Journal of Psychiatry* 148:365–370.

Christenson, G. A., R. L. Pyle, and J. E. Mitchell. 1991. "Estimated lifetime prevalence of trichotillomania in college students." *Journal of Clinical Psychiatry* 52:415–417.

Cohen, L. J., D. J. Stein, D. Simeon, E. Spadaccini, J. Rosen, B. Aronowitz, and E. Hollander. 1995. "Clinical profile, comorbidity, and treatment history in 123 hair pullers: a survey study." *Journal of Clinical Psychiatry* 56:319–326.

Davis, H. 1914. "Epidemic alopecia areata." *British Journal of Dermatology* 26:207–210.

Gluhoski, V. L. 1995. "A cognitive approach for treating trichotillomania." *Journal of Psychotherapy Practice and Research* 4:277–285.

Golomb, R. G., and S. M. Vavrichek. 1999. *The Hairpulling Habit and You: How to Solve the Trichotillomania Puzzle.* Silver Spring, Md.: Writers' Cooperative of Greater Washington.

Greenberg, H. R., and C. A. Sarner. 1965. "Trichotillomania: symptom and syndrome." *Archives of General Psychiatry* 12:482–489.

Hallopeau, M. 1889. "Alopecie par grattage (trichomanie ou trichotillomanie)." *Annales de Dermatologie et de Syphiligraphie* 10:440–441.

Keuthen, N. J., R. L. O'Sullivan, P. Goodchild, D. Rodriguez, M. Jenike, and L. Baer. 1998. "Retrospective review of treatment outcome for 63 patients with trichotillomania." *American Journal of Psychiatry* 155:560–561.

Keuthen, N. J., R. L. O'Sullivan, C. F. Hayday, K. E. Peets, M. A. Jenike, and L. Baer. 1997. "The relationship of menstrual cycle and pregnancy to compulsive hairpulling." *Psychotherapy and Psychosomatics* 66:33–37.

Keuthen, N. J., R. L. O'Sullivan, J. N. Ricciardi, D. Shera, C. Savage, A. S. Borgmann, M. Jenike, and L. Baer. 1995. "The Massachusetts General Hospital (MGH) Hairpulling Scale, I: Development and factor analysis." *Psychotherapy and Psychosomatics* 64:141–145.

Koblenzer, C. S. 1987. *Psychocutaneous Disease.* New York, N.Y.: Grune and Stratton.

Lang, A., W. Leaf, and E. Myers (translators). 1945. *The Iliad of Homer.* Abridged and edited by W. B. Moffett. New York: Macmillan.

Lenane, M. C., S. E. Swedo, J. L. Rapoport, H. Leonard, W. Sceery, and J. Guroff. 1992. "Rates of obsessive compulsive disorder in first degree relatives of patients with trichotillomania: a research note." *Journal of Child Psychology and Psychiatry* 33:925–933.

Leonard, H. L., S. E. Swedo, J. L. Rapoport, E. V. Koby, M. C. Lenane, D. L. Cheslow, and S. W. Hamburger. 1989. "Treatment of childhood obsessive-compulsive disorder with clomipramine and desipramine: a double-blind crossover comparison." *Archives of General Psychiatry* 46:1088–1092.

O'Sullivan, R. L., N. J. Keuthen, and G. Gumley. 1996. "Trichotillomania and carpal tunnel syndrome." *Journal of Clinical Psychiatry* 57:174.

O'Sullivan, R. L., S. L. Rauch, H. C. Breiter, I. D. Grachev, L. Baer, D. N. Kennedy, N. J. Keuthen, P. A. Manzo, V. S. Caviness, and M. A. Jenike. 1997. "Reduced basal ganglia volumes in trichotillomania measured by morphometric magnetic resonance imaging." *Biological Psychiatry* 42:39–45.

Rapoport J. L. 1989. *The Boy Who Couldn't Stop Washing.* New York: E. P. Dutton.

Rothbaum, B. O., L. Shaw, R. Morris, and P. T. Ninan. 1993. "Prevalence of trichotillomania in a college freshman population" [letter]. *Journal of Clinical Psychiatry* 54:72.

Soriano, J. L., R. L. O'Sullivan, L. Baer, K. A. Phillips, R. J. McNally, and M. A. Jenike. 1996. "Trichotillomania and self-esteem: a survey of 62 female hair pullers." *Journal of Clinical Psychiatry* 57:77–82.

Stanley, M. A., J. W. Borden, G. E. Bell, and A. L. Wagner. 1994. "Nonclinical hair-pulling: phenomenology and related psychopathology." *Journal of Anxiety Disorders* 8:119–130.

Stein, D. J., D. Wessels, J. Carr, S. Hawkridge, C. Bouwer, and N. Kalis. 1997. "Hair-pulling in a patient with Sydenham's chorea" (letter). *American Journal of Psychiatry* 154:1320.

Swedo, S. E., M. C. Lenane, and H. L. Leonard. 1993. "Long-term treatment of trichotillomania (hair pulling)." *New England Journal of Medicine* 329:141–142.

Swedo, S. E., H. L. Leonard, M. C. Lenane, and D. C. Rettew. 1992. "Trichotillomania. A profile of the disorder from infancy through adulthood." *International Pediatrics* 7:144–150.

Swedo, S. E., H. L. Leonard, J. L. Rapoport, M. C. Lenane, E. L. Goldberger, and D. L. Cheslow. 1989. "A double blind comparison of clomipramine and desipramine in the treatment of trichotillomania (hair pulling)." *New England Journal of Medicine* 321:497–501.

Swedo, S. E., J. L. Rapoport, D. L. Cheslow, H. L. Leonard, E. M. Ayoub, D. M. Hosier, and E. R. Wald. 1989. "High prevalence of obsessive-compulsive symptoms in patients with Sydenham's chorea." *American Journal of Psychiatry* 146:246–249.

Swedo, S. E., J. L. Rapoport, H. L. Leonard, M. B. Schapiro, S. I. Rapoport, and C. L. Grady. 1991. "Regional cerebral glucose metabolism of women with trichotillomania." *Archives of General Psychiatry* 48:828–833.

Watson, T. S. and K. D. Allen. 1993. "Elimination of thumb-sucking as a treatment for severe trichotillomania." *Journal of the American Academy of Child and Adolescent Psychiatry* 42:1171–1174.

Recommended Readings

Anders, J. L., and J. W. Jefferson. 1998. *Trichotillomania. A Guide.* Revised Edition. Madison, Wis.: Obsessive-Compulsive Information Center, Madison Institute of Medicine.

Baer, L. 2000. *Getting Control. Overcoming Your Obsessions and Compulsions.* Revised Edition. New York: Dutton.

Golomb, R. G., and S. M. Vavrichek. 1999. *The Hairpulling Habit and You: How to Solve the Trichotillomania Puzzle.* Silver Spring, Md.: Writers' Cooperative of Greater Washington.

Penzel, F. 2000. *Obsessive-Compulsive Disorders: A Complete Guide to Getting Well and Staying Well.* New York: Oxford University Press.

Salazar, C. 1995. *You Are Not Alone. Compulsive Hair Pulling: The Enemy Within.* Sacramento, Calif.: Rophe Press.

Stein, D. J, G. A. Christenson, and E. Hollander. 1999. *Trichotillomania.* Washington, D.C.: American Psychiatric Press, Inc.

(Note: The publications listed are either exclusively on trichotillomania or on OCD with sections on trichotillomania.)

Dr. Nancy J. Keuthen is Co-Director of the Trichotillomania Clinic and Chief Psychologist of the Obsessive-Compulsive Disorders Clinic and Research Unit at Massachusetts General Hospital. She is also an assistant professor of psychology at Harvard Medical School. Dr. Keuthen has evaluated and treated hundreds of hair pullers in her multidisciplinary clinic and sponsored numerous conferences and symposia on this topic. She is a member (and previous vice-chair) of the scientific board of the Trichotillomania Learning Center. She has authored numerous scientific papers in this field including the longitudinal outcome of treatment for trichotillomania, neuropsychological functioning in individuals with trichotillomania, and premenstrual exacerbations of hair pulling symptoms. She has also developed and published the only self-report assessment scale for this disorder.

Dan Stein, M.D., is Research Associate Professor of Psychiatry at the University of Florida, Gainesville, and Director of the MRC Research Unit on Anxiety Disorders at the University of Stellenbosch in Cape Town, South Africa. The former Director of Anxiety Disorders and Assistant Professor of Clinical Psychiatry at Mt. Sinai Medical School and New York's Queens Hospital, Dr. Stein has treated many Trichotillomania patients, and contributed to numerous original research papers on the subject. He is the coeditor, among other books on compulsive and impulsive disorders, of *Trichotillomania*, and a Member of the Scientific Advisory Board of the Trichotillomania Learning Center.

Gary A. Christenson, M.D., is the Director of Mental Health at the University of Minnesota's Boynton Health Service. He is also an Associate Clinical Professor of Psychiatry at the University of Minnesota Medical School. Dr. Christenson has treated hundreds of Trichotillomania sufferers, has published widely on the subject, and is a co-editor to *Trichotillomania*.

Some Other New Harbinger Self-Help Titles

Family Guide to Emotional Wellness, $24.95
Undefended Love, $13.95
The Great Big Book of Hope, $15.95
Don't Leave it to Chance, $13.95
Emotional Claustrophobia, $12.95
The Relaxation & Stress Reduction Workbook, Fifth Edition, $19.95
The Loneliness Workbook, $14.95
Thriving with Your Autoimmune Disorder, $16.95
Illness and the Art of Creative Self-Expression, $13.95
The Interstitial Cystitis Survival Guide, $14.95
Outbreak Alert, $15.95
Don't Let Your Mind Stunt Your Growth, $10.95
Energy Tapping, $14.95
Under Her Wing, $13.95
Self-Esteem, Third Edition, $15.95
Women's Sexualitites, $15.95
Knee Pain, $14.95
Helping Your Anxious Child, $12.95
Breaking the Bonds of Irritable Bowel Syndrome, $14.95
Multiple Chemical Sensitivity: A Survival Guide, $16.95
Dancing Naked, $14.95
Why Are We Still Fighting, $15.95
From Sabotage to Success, $14.95
Parkinson's Disease and the Art of Moving, $15.95
A Survivor's Guide to Breast Cancer, $13.95
Men, Women, and Prostate Cancer, $15.95
Make Every Session Count: Getting the Most Out of Your Brief Therapy, $10.95
Virtual Addiction, $12.95
After the Breakup, $13.95
Why Can't I Be the Parent I Want to Be?, $12.95
The Secret Message of Shame, $13.95
The OCD Workbook, $18.95
Tapping Your Inner Strength, $13.95
Binge No More, $14.95
When to Forgive, $12.95
Practical Dreaming, $12.95
Healthy Baby, Toxic World, $15.95
Making Hope Happen, $14.95
I'll Take Care of You, $12.95
Survivor Guilt, $14.95
Children Changed by Trauma, $13.95
Understanding Your Child's Sexual Behavior, $12.95
The Self-Esteem Companion, $10.95
The Gay and Lesbian Self-Esteem Book, $13.95
Making the Big Move, $13.95
How to Survive and Thrive in an Empty Nest, $13.95
Living Well with a Hidden Disability, $15.95
Overcoming Repetitive Motion Injuries the Rossiter Way, $15.95
What to Tell the Kids About Your Divorce, $13.95
The Divorce Book, Second Edition, $15.95
Claiming Your Creative Self: True Stories from the Everyday Lives of Women, $15.95
Taking Control of TMJ, $13.95
Winning Against Relapse: A Workbook of Action Plans for Recurring Health and Emotional Problems, $14.95
Facing 30: Women Talk About Constructing a Real Life and Other Scary Rites of Passage, $12.95
The Worry Control Workbook, $15.95
Wanting What You Have: A Self-Discovery Workbook, $18.95
When Perfect Isn't Good Enough: Strategies for Coping with Perfectionism, $13.95
Earning Your Own Respect: A Handbook of Personal Responsibility, $12.95
High on Stress: A Woman's Guide to Optimizing the Stress in Her Life, $13.95
Infidelity: A Survival Guide, $13.95
Stop Walking on Eggshells, $14.95
Consumer's Guide to Psychiatric Drugs, $16.95
The Fibromyalgia Advocate: Getting the Support You Need to Cope with Fibromyalgia and Myofascial Pain, $18.95
Working Anger: Preventing and Resolving Conflict on the Job, $12.95
Healthy Living with Diabetes, $13.95
Better Boundries: Owning and Treasuring Your Life, $13.95
Goodbye Good Girl, $12.95
Fibromyalgia & Chronic Myofascial Pain Syndrome, $19.95
The Depression Workbook: Living With Depression and Manic Depression, $17.95